Running on Full

To Tricia + Bill Walker. Best Wishes. Neil Wilkinson

Running on Full
The Story of Ruth and Ruby Crawford

by
Neil Wilkinson

The Kennesaw State University Press

The Kennesaw State University Press
Kennesaw, Georgia USA

Published by The Kennesaw State University Press
Kennesaw State University
1000 Chastain Road
MD 2701
Kennesaw, GA 30144

Holly S. Miller, Cover & Book Design, Production Editor

Volkmer, Bill. (Copyright holder). (1999). Atlanta Trolley and Streetcar Photos, [Online Image]. Retrieved October 15, 2006, from Bill Volkmer Collection Web Site: http://www.davesrailpix.com/index.html

Georgia Public Television (Producer), & Kennedy D. (Host). Aired 1999, and 2001. *Lost Atlanta: The Way We Were* ©1994: United States: Georgia Public Broadcasting. (Graciously made available on DVD by Georgia Public Television, 2007.)

Mary Mac's Tea Room photographs reproduced by Haigwood Studios, Roswell, Georgia.

Library of Congress Cataloging-in-Publication Data

Wilkinson, Neil, 1952-
Running on Full : The Story of Ruth and Ruby Crawford / by Neil Wilkinson.
p. cm.
Includes bibliographical references.
ISBN 978-1-933483-23-8
1. Crawford, Ruth, d. 2005. 2. Crawford, Ruby, d. 2009. 3. Atlanta (Ga.)--Biography. 4. Businesswomen--Georgia--Atlanta--Biography. 5. Civic leaders--Georgia--Atlanta--Biography. 6. Volunteers--Georgia--Atlanta--Biography. 7. Twins--Georgia--Atlanta--Biography. 8. Community life--Georgia--Atlanta--History. 9. Atlanta (Ga.)--Social life and customs--20th century. 10. Temple (Ga.)--Biography. I. Title.
F294.A853C739 2009
975.8'0430922--dc22
[B]
2009028903

Printed in the United States of America
10 9 8 7 6 5 4 3 2

From Ruby

Dedicated to the Loving Memory
of
My Beloved Twin Ruth Marian Crawford

And Our Parents
Elizabeth Lois Gray Crawford and William Hampton Crawford
Who taught us to work, to like to work, and by example, how to live.

From the Author

To Nanny and Dad

Contents

Foreword

On October 3, 2005, eleven months after this project began, Ruth Crawford, beloved sister and identical twin of Ruby Crawford, passed this life after courageously and tenaciously battling her final illness. Ruth was, and in her own special way still is, a gracious and generous participant in the creation of this book, just as she was a gracious and generous participant in every facet of her too-short life. This account was underway when Ruth's health prevented her active participation in the project, an eventuality that Ruby reported as a disappointment to Ruth because it represented unfinished business, a condition not at all synonymous with Ruth Crawford.

As the circumstances of Ruth's death had to be dealt with, Ruby did so. She was as generous with her time as she could be. We worked on this book between trips, hospital stays, stints in rehabilitation after surgery, and so on. As Ruby's eyesight began to wane, something that cost her a driver's license, something that bothered her mightily, she continued to motor on as she had before, only in someone else's car, to every event she could.

Ruby, speaking publicly for the first time after Ruth's passing, had this to say: There's still a lot to do, so I guess I'll just have to do double duty now." Indeed, for as much her failing health allowed her, she continued doing double duty.

Ruby Crawford departed this life on June 6, 2009. She will, like her sister Ruth, be sorely missed and fondly and lovingly remembered by all who had the pleasure of knowing her. By Ruby's last Summer of 2008, she and I developed a special relationship that is one of the most special it has ever been my privilege to be a part of.

A substantial portion of the following text was taken from conversations with Ruth and Ruby, in person or by telephone. Many comments, stories, anecdotes, and the like appear in the present tense, having been recorded and transcribed as they were told to preserve the spontaneity, humor, and the unique voices of these two remarkable women. This Foreword is offered to relieve any confusion that might arise as to continuity.

Quite often the Crawford sisters responded to inquiries in tandem, a characteristic of siblings, twins especially. Ruth might begin an answer and Ruby might finish it, or Ruby began and Ruth finished. In those cases, quotes are presented as composites attributed to both ladies. When one speaks individually, that too is noted. A conversation with Ruth and Ruby together was a shared experience of talking with three entities, the individual women, Ruth

Crawford and Ruby Crawford, and that third element that was the Crawford Twins, the sisterhood where attribution is unnecessary or obtrusive.

The one important characteristic of any conversation with either or both sisters that is nearly impossible to convey elegantly on the page is that most of what Ruth and Ruby had to say about themselves, their lives, accomplishments, and events of impact on their lives was accompanied by infectious laughter and endless smiles. Unwieldy attributions and clumsy notations are inadequate tools to share accurately with the reader what a conversation with the Crawford sisters was really like. Laughter rolled like cool, sweet spring water, most of it directed at themselves. For as seriously as they took life, faith, family, service, achievement, and stewardship, as well as the people who helped them along the way, the Crawford sisters themselves were not among the things either took very seriously at all. As a result, Ruth and Ruby often became their own greatest source of fun and amusement, a refreshing thing indeed.

Ruth and Ruby Crawford, as busy "retired" as at any time in their lives, were kind enough to meet for a series of talks. Our first was at The Varsity, the original in downtown Atlanta, where they were very well known and greatly admired. The Varsity, an Atlanta landmark famous for its chili dogs, fried pies, and Frosted Orange, has always been a favorite of the Crawford sisters, who ordered their Slaw Dogs that day "all the way."

Throughout our talks, Ruth and Ruby were gracious and generous in making themselves available when their busy schedule allowed, up to and including assuring me that I could call them at any time of the day or night: "We don't go to bed until two or three in the morning," the ladies told me, "Late's when we do all our reading. So you can call then, if you need to." I never did so, not because I doubted the sincerity of the invitation, but because I can't stay up as late as the Crawford sisters did.

This chronicle is a condensation of many interviews, meetings, and phone conversations with one or both of the ladies that included a show and tell of photos, newspaper clippings, magazine articles, and other material that the Crawford ladies graciously made available from their personal archives. The interviews, discussions, and meetings took place at various times over a period of nearly four years, yet little attention is paid to when any particular conversation took place, as temporal placement is unnecessary in most cases, except in the broadest sense. Their story is told against the backdrop of the many and monumental changes that took place in the world, America, Georgia, Atlanta, and Temple, all quite important in order to in understand Ruth and Ruby, and to have some appreciation for the times in which they lived.

Running on Full is the account of those times, and the sisters' accomplishments, recollections, and observations of them. Ruth and Ruby Crawford, twin sisters from Temple, Georgia arrived in Atlanta in early 1943, bubbling over with talent, drive, and ability. With infectious curiosity, endless enthusiasm, and bags of style and charm, they brought with them a work ethic that seemed to know no bounds and that was instilled in them from their most tender years. These ingredients propelled them to seek and meet challenges virtually unheard of for women in that era and in the decades following. They sought and met those challenges filled always to capacity with an unwavering faith and a strong spiritual grounding that translated not only into professional successes and recognition, but into a chronicle of stewardship, community service, and civic responsibility, and pride that was simply extraordinary. Ruth and Ruby Crawford embodied an abiding and moving love for humanity and compassion for those in need that was as real as it was beautiful.

For those people who had empty places, voids, and hollow spots in their lives, whether someone was in need of something as simple though substantial as a meal, someone in a nursing home needing to see a friendly face, or any of the many service and civic organizations in which they served, Ruth and Ruby were able to take from their vast and seemingly endless store of faith, hope, charity, and enormous reserves of humor, ingenuity, and energy to offer those things to others unselfishly and unswervingly, and yet they were diminished not in the least, but renewed, and with such service their own tanks were continually refilled.

It is in this service to a community of people who were often "running on empty" that these two women selflessly dedicated themselves from the time they were very young, all while working diligently on their own relationships, growth, careers, and accomplishments. What is more, they did everything they did cheerfully, tirelessly, and abundantly, in effect, Running on Full, with full hearts, full minds, and full spirits.

Prologue

The Race

The problem with doing nothing is that you never know
when you're done.

-Ruth and Ruby Crawford

A nd then, just like that, they came. The sustained thrum from the
thousands lining the street increased, then changed abruptly to a steady
cheer. What had an instant before been the very unusual scene of Atlanta's
Peachtree Road clear of traffic was gone. Like a flood down a narrow valley, the
first wave of black-clad Kenyans and other serious racers filled the street and
flashed past. And then, one by one, in twos, three, fours, and more, runners
stopped, to shake hands, embrace, introduce children and friends, and have
pictures made with the two smiling and colorful ladies, twin sisters, dressed
in identical red, white, and blue outfits, complete with patriotic hats, waving
the Stars and Stripes over the throng passing in review.

The 2005 Peachtree Road Race happened on a humid, much-cooler-than-
normal day under an overcast sky. In attendance on the curb at 3180 Peachtree
Road, the address of Peachtree Road United Methodist Church, in their festive
matching outfits complete with stylishly foreshortened Uncle Sam hats, Ruth
and Ruby Crawford, as they had every Fourth of July for thirty-five previous
races, waved and smiled at the racers.

Waves and smiles are as much a part of Ruth and Ruby Crawford as
peaches and peanuts are a part of Georgia. And Ruth and Ruby are as much a
part of Georgia as red clay and Stone Mountain.

"I wasn't all for it in the beginning," Ruby recalls. "We started going the
second year they had the race. We had just moved out Peachtree Road to
Narmore Drive right past Lenox near where the race begins. That year, Ruth
dragged me out of bed the first time, I said, 'Why do you think that we have to
get up at this ungodly hour to get out and see that bunch run down Peachtree
Road?' and she said, 'To encourage them; to spur them on.' We had such a
good time that we never missed another one."

"I was so sleepy, I kept thinking, 'What are we doing up at this hour?'
We had to leave our house no later than six o'clock. Otherwise we wouldn't

have been able to get out of our own driveway and up the street to the church where we always watched it. I just thought it was so awful to get up at that early hour and go out. But we had so much fun, and then it just turned into something special. It was, as some people like to joke and call it, 'the Ruth and Ruby Road Race.'"

Who are these ladies who are greeted by so many–hundreds and more–from the race? Who are they who prompt so many to stop racing, cameras in hand, to thank, to kiss, to hug, and to pose for pictures with them?

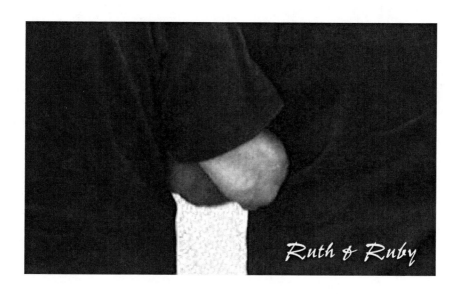

Ruth & Ruby

Chapter One

The Homeplace

Home is where the heart is and hence a movable feast.
—Angela Carter

Temple, Georgia, settled seventeen years after the conclusion of the Civil War, is similar to many very small towns, the kind native Southerners refer to as "little small" or "small little." The nagging question and running discussion of which is the smaller of the two enlivens many a reminiscence of the way things were only a generation or two ago.

A bit more awkwardly bisected by the railroad than many of her counterparts across the South, Temple fits into that category of town that sprang up to straddle railroad tracks coursing the state. The main road through Temple, U.S. 78, and the railroad parallel one another as they cut their angular tandem course east to west through its heart where the town acquiesces to the contours of the land. Temple's central and southern portions rest on higher ground than the northern end of town. The topography is terraced by the upper village, the roadbeds of the highway and the railroad, and the lower end where the land flattens at a row of buildings attached to one another like sisters holding hands.

Many towns throughout the South share with Temple the lonesome, used-up garages, stores, warehouses, and churches whose customers and congregations have moved on or passed on. Warped planks still hold a bit of pigment from their last painting or are tinted a pale orange by the dust from Georgia clay. On the sides of buildings, faded lettering for cigarette ads, insurance agencies, funeral services, and various mercantile interests testifies to a more vibrant time in the life of the town. Temple is a town, like Millen, Rockmart, Folkston, or Darien, that decades ago was much busier, much more self-contained and self-sufficient, more populous, with more going concerns, and few, if any, lonely buildings. That was before there were interstate highways, retailing giants, the flight of jobs to cities, and subdivisions sprouting everywhere like mushrooms after a warm rain.

Shown on the old census maps as "Temple Village," the town is located at the western edge of Carroll County and sits on a grand total of 6.8 square miles. It is forty-five miles from Atlanta, and the last Census in 2000 shows its population of 2,383 divided roughly equally by gender, the slight majority of its citizens being women. Now, the dominant structures in the old town are a water tower and the steeple of the red brick Methodist church. Interstate 20 crosses the southern end of the new City of Temple that has grown out to meet the big highway. Out there are new municipal buildings, retail outlets, shiny storefronts, and other signs of vitality and growth. The old town still stands, and it is from that little small or small little town of Temple, Georgia, that Ruth and Ruby Crawford emerged in 1943 Atlanta to begin their careers.

"In those days, our day," Ruby tells, recalling some of old downtown Temple's former vitality, "Temple had two banks, and that was pretty good for a small town, and Temple was very small. When we were growing up there were probably between three and four hundred people living in town. By the time Ruth and I came to Atlanta, Temple had about seven hundred and twenty people. That was in 1943."

"That one strip along the railroad track that has gotten so run down in the last several years, dilapidated really, was the center of things. They're building out by the highway and the truck stops instead of uptown, now. But they have started a program to try to revitalize the downtown."

"We lived in the third house out of town on the Villa Rica Highway. It was situated so that we could walk nearly everywhere we went in Temple."

"There were about twelve stores all told," Ruth added. "There were the bank buildings and a drug store and then across the road we had the Williams manufacturing plant that built breakfast room sets. Stevens built cabinets for kitchens and homes. Oh, and we had two cotton gins in town. One of them also sold coal and wood to people for heating. And that was just about it. Except for the railroad. The railroad was a big part of the town back then. It runs right through the middle of town, you know."

"Oh yes," Ruby recalled, "We had that little train called Accommodation. Nothing was ever more appropriately named, because it came through town at about seven o'clock in the morning and people rode it to Atlanta to go to school and to work, and it left Atlanta about 5:30 in the afternoon, so they'd quit their day's work and ride it back home. All the people out in Austell and Temple, Douglasville, Carrollton, Bremen, and Tallapoosa called it Accommodation because that was really what it was. It accommodated so many people. Of course the Southern, the Southern Railway that went to Washington and New York, came through Temple. We had a depot back then, and we actually had a hotel across from the depot. Dr. Pierce Harris's mother-in-law and daddy-in-law ran the hotel. We had a restaurant and grocery store, so the traveling salesmen—they called them drummers back in those days—would get off the train and go over to the hotel right across the street and check in. Our daddy ran a little taxi service—they called them jitneys back then."

"Daddy and Dr. Spruill had the first T-model Fords in Temple," Ruth recalled. "I remember how excited we used to be to get a new T-model Ford, just as excited as I would be with a new Cadillac now. When the salesmen finished there in Temple, they'd want to go to Bremen or Carrollton, and Daddy would take them in the jitney."

"In those days," she continued, "we didn't have big car dealerships like we did later on. The salesmen would come through town, show off the cars, well, the car anyway, there was only the one. Just the T-model. Then he'd write up his orders if he had any and move on."

"We used to get a kick out of the slogan that supposedly came from Henry Ford—that you could have any car you wanted as long as it was a T-model—"

"And any color you wanted as long as it was black."

Ruth and Ruby grew up in the 1920s as Georgia was emerging from Reconstruction, the Agrarian Rebellion, and World War I. Cotton, as it had been for much of the State's history, was still the most important crop in Georgia, and prices peaked in 1919, collapsed quickly, and remained depressed for years after. Temple, like most farming communities in Georgia, felt those changes that saw the beginnings of the financial difficulties, dislocations, and losses that would plague the State and the country well into the 1930s.

This was the time of the boll weevil, an infestation that could destroy a year's cotton crop in a few short weeks. Farmers all over the South were ruined by *anthonomus grandis*, a beetle that lay dormant in winter and emerged to devour cotton buds and flowers in Spring, forcing cotton farmers to let sharecroppers and farmhands go, creating even greater unemployment, poverty, and a migration from Georgia to points north where jobs could be found. The boll weevil was so reviled that to adults of the day, like Ruth and Ruby's parents, referring to someone as a boll weevil was an insult of high degree, indicating a person of shifty and worthless character.

The Atlanta Ruth and Ruby knew as girls and young women was nothing like Atlanta today. To anyone who has moved to the Atlanta area in the last twenty years or so, as have a sizeable portion of the more than 4,000,000 people who now populate the metropolitan area, there is an underlying sense of having missed something.

"There was a small town atmosphere then," the sisters recalled, "everyone seemed to know everyone else. Of course, we didn't know them all, but it seemed that way. It's not that way anymore."

Whenever an Atlanta native is encountered, an occurrence becoming more rare by the day, there is a temptation to grab a camera and quickly record the event for posterity. Should two such people come within earshot, listen carefully as the banter turns almost immediately to the sort of thing expected at a school reunion. There is a sense that things were different in Atlanta not all that long ago, and a sense that things have changed forever. Natives and long-time residents speak of Atlanta as a long lost friend, and many of those speakers are unfamiliar with this city as it is now. There is always a lot of "Whatever happened to …?" or "Do you remember when …?" going on between natives and long-timers who happen to cross paths and start to remember how things were, who "your people were," and what happened to the small town feeling that was once Atlanta.

Atlanta has grown and extended her reach to the point that "little old Temple" is now a part of the Metropolitan Statistical Area (MSA) that constitutes modern Greater Atlanta. The United States Office of Management and Budget records that the MSA for Atlanta comprises 19 counties. Growth in the region has been steady and enormous. To a great degree impervious to economic downturns that have plagued many areas of the country, Atlanta has experienced some growth every year since the end of the Civil War.

Even in tough economic times, Atlanta and its surrounding communities have enjoyed relatively stable employment, steady but not inflationary real property appreciation, and one of the most attractive sites in the country for locating a business's regional or headquarters offices.

When the Crawford sisters were just toddlers, Thomas W. Hardwick, who had served in the U. S. House and Senate, was elected Governor of Georgia and held the office from 1921 until 1923, during which time Georgia's U.S.

Senator, Thomas E. Watson, died. In a move that was as progressive for its time as it was prophetic for the Crawford sisters, Governor Hardwick appointed Rebecca Latimer Felton to the Senate as Watson's replacement, making her the first woman to serve as a U.S. Senator.

Over in Atlanta, where two short but very eventful decades later Ruth and Ruby would go, James L. Key was serving his first two terms as Mayor, beginning in 1918. He would eventually serve four terms and be the driving force behind the formation of Atlanta's first City Planning Commission and the building of the Spring Street Viaduct. He opposed Prohibition, the banning of Sunday baseball games and movies under the State's Blue Laws, and oversaw improvements to Atlanta's sewer system, Municipal Auditorium, and the Cyclorama. During Mayor Key's second tenure Atlanta's African-American population began to flex its political muscle for the first time, an event that would have lasting effects on Atlanta, the state, and the country.

In the years between Key's first and last terms as mayor, Walter Sims was elected to the office. It was Mayor Sims who dispatched a very young alderman, William B. Hartsfield, who would later become a great friend of Ruth and Ruby, to determine a good location for an airport to serve Atlanta, an initiative that would forever change Atlanta and Georgia. Candler Field, south of the City, was chosen and a deal struck with the City in 1925 to lease the land for the project. The following year the U.S. Mail began service to and from the airport, portending Atlanta's future as the aerial crossroads of the Southeast.

It was in these years and through the 1930s that Ruth and Ruby, in the company of their mother and father, visited Atlanta quite often. The city was a growing, sprawling place, full of wagons, trolleys, and whistles clattering, clanging, and caterwauling. It was a place Ruth and Ruby loved when they were girls and a time that they recalled with great fondness.

On the national front, events transpired that affected the Crawford family every bit as much they affected other families in Georgia, the South, and around the country. The decade of the 1920s, "The Roaring Twenties," saw Prohibition and the rise of organized crime centered around bootleg whiskey, which in an economically depressed South had its own special effects when hard-pressed Southerners needed to feed their families.

The country had four Presidents in eleven years. Woodrow Wilson was followed by Warren G. Harding, who died in office and was succeeded by Calvin Coolidge. Coolidge's brand of laissez-faire government has been cited as a major cause of the Depression. He was succeeded by Herbert Hoover. Rural and small town America, and Temple was no exception, suffered serious economic conditions while the rest of the country, big cities primarily, appeared prosperous. Hoover's "Efficiency Movement" was met head on by the Great Depression, a result that had profound effects on the Crawford sisters when they were growing up and, like many who grew up in that era, for the remainder of their lives.

All was not gloom and doom, though. The great sports figures of the day were people like Bobby Jones. The Atlanta golfing legend held all four major titles in that era, The U.S. Open, The U. S. Amateur, The British Amateur, and The British Open. Babe Ruth was the Sultan of Swat, hitting home runs as regularly as he struck out. The Twenties roared, movies began to talk, politics were, as always, robust, and things were happening all over America.

—

Always tell the truth,
but don't always be telling it.

Emily Post's popular manual *Etiquette in Society, in Business, in Politics and at Home* appeared in 1922, making Ms. Post a household word for the next five decades and providing useful and interesting reading for young women like the Crawford girls. Among the axioms Ruth and Ruby put into practice all their lives was Miss Post's oft-repeated philosophy that, "Manners are a sensitive awareness of the feelings of others. If you have that awareness, you have good manners, no matter what fork you use."

—

It's better to be ignorant
than to say what ain't so.

Chapter Two

Our Li'l Ol' Daddy

If I have seen farther than others, it is because I have
stood on the shoulders of giants.
—Sir Isaac Newton

O ver a hot dog lunch at The Varsity, the Atlanta drive-in with the unique
atmosphere of railroad station curio shop, Big Top circus, and high-
efficiency dispensary of Slaw Dogs, Fried Pies, and Frosted Orange drinks,
Ruth and Ruby recalled their childhood in Temple.

"Our daddy was William Hampton Crawford," Ruth began, "but
everybody called him Dad Crawford. So since it was not unusual for him
to be called Dad, we shortened his given names and we called him Willie
Hamp. And he liked it."

"Everybody called him Dad Crawford," Ruby says, "except his two darlin'
little twin girls."

"Daddy thought his 'darling duo,' as he liked to call us, could do no wrong.
But he was married to a lady who thought otherwise", Ruth added.

"I recall once when we were grown and living in Atlanta that we had been
to the Georgia Bar's Mid-Winter party in Atlanta. After the party we headed
straight out to Temple late that Friday evening. We got there after Mother and
Daddy had gone to bed. When we went to take our coats off, Mother could see
in the triple mirror between their room and mine that I had on a dress with a
low-cut neckline, nothing immodest, you know, just the fashion of the day. It
was one of those dresses that we liked to say makes the 'torso more so.' Well
don't you know, Mother called me into her room and said, 'Ruby did anyone
else come to the party naked besides you two?' Daddy was next to her in bed
just laughing his head off. I'm not sure I found it all that amusing."

"I'm pretty sure Mama never slept a wink that night, because the next
morning she was ready for us again. She wanted to know why in the world we
would go out dressed like that. She said, 'I thought I'd taught you both better
than that.'"

"Daddy just sat there laughing about the whole thing, and there we were
grown women, members in good standing of the State Bar of Georgia, with
good responsible jobs, living on our own in the big city of Atlanta, still being

disciplined by Mama. Oh, she was so upset with us, and there's our li'l ol' daddy doubled over laughing at all three of us."

"What we did know was that when we were girls our mother was one of those ladies who truly believed that old saying that 'idle hands are the devil's workshop.'" She kept us so busy that we would never have had any time to get into any trouble, had we been so inclined."

"Mama was a woman who knew only one punctuation mark—a period. No exclamation points, no semi-colons, no questions marks. When she said something that was it—no discussion, no controversy, no questions—period."

"Whenever Ruth or I wanted to do something Mama didn't think we ought to be doing, even when we were well grown, she would demand to know, 'Don't you have a lick of sense?' I remember telling her one time that 'believe it or not, in some circles I am thought of as highly intelligent.' She just looked at me and asked, 'Which ones?'"

"I remember once when were little girls, maybe four or five years old, we had a neighbor, Ms. Eula Wren, who just loved all the neighborhood kids. Well Ms. Wren had invited us to come for lunch one day and we were so excited. So Mama scrubbed us clean and shined us up like we'd been done up with Johnson's Glo-Coat."

"Before we left Mama told us three things we were to remember no matter what. The first was that when we got to the railroad tracks that run through the middle of Temple we were to look both ways and we were not to cross under any circumstances if we could see the train. The second one was that we were to wash our hands before we ate, and the third and most important one was that we were to thank Ms. Eula for our lunch."

"So we set off to Ms. Eula's, holding hands and saying those three things over and over to make sure we had them just right. We were so wound up by the time we got to Ms. Wren's house wanting to do just what Mama told us that when Ms. Wren opened the door we blurted out our thanks for lunch before we'd even been invited in. For years after that, every time we saw her, Ms. Wren would tease us no end about that."

"Ruth and I always liked to get things done, and we always wanted to do whatever Mama told us. So there we were when Ms. Wren opened that door just singing our thanks, and she had yet to even open the screen door."

"Mama laid down the law to us so often that when we went to law school we thought our admission to the bar would be just a formality. We thought it ought to have been automatic."

"She wasn't mean to us, don't you know, but she was strict. Daddy was much more easy-going and affable. That made for a good balance between them. It must have, because they were married for sixty-one years. And Daddy looked after her so tenderly and lovingly all of those years."

"Daddy was from Temple. Mother was Elizabeth Lois Gray Crawford. We called her Queen Elizabeth. She was from Temple, too. They were both born right there in Temple."

"We had an older brother," Ruth recounted, "Dayton Hampton Crawford, who was twelve years old when we were born and is now deceased, and a sister, Mary Elizabeth."

"Joan."

"She changed her name to Joan. She was named Mary Elizabeth."

"She was five years old when we were born."

"Our brother adored us. He was like a second father to us."

The sisters laughed when they recalled, "But our five-year-old sister did not like us at all."

"She stood out in front of the house and tried to give us away to everyone who passed the house, asking them if they didn't want some little old twin babies. But no one did. I'm not sure that Mother and Daddy did either, but they were stuck with us," they laughed in agreement, and said, "That's the reason we tell everybody that we came into this world unwanted, and it warped our personalities."

"Our li'l ol' daddy always said that he was sure the stork meant to make a delivery at the John D. Rockefeller house, but guessed that with his heavy load the stork had to make a forced landing at the Crawford household in Temple, Georgia."

"Later on, when we were grown, he would say that we had champagne tastes …"

"… and a beer income."

If there are any two people in the lives of Ruth and Ruby Crawford who occupy the pinnacle, those two people would be their parents. Rare is the conversation with either lady that does not include a lesson, an anecdote, or a fond memory of Elizabeth or William Hampton Crawford. Equally rare is it to hear either woman take much credit for her own personal accomplishments, favoring instead, as explanation for their boundless energy, layered and multiple careers, astonishing work ethic, grace, and civic stewardship, the examples set by "Mother" and "Daddy."

Family lore and personal memories pour easily from the Crawford ladies. "Daddy grew up on a sixty-acre farm. Mother grew up on a forty-acre farm. They were not adjacent, but not many miles apart. Daddy eventually bought both of them. He owned the farms and he also had a grocery store in Temple as well as our home, and then we had a business."

"When Daddy started out his little business, he milked the cows and brought in the milk. Every day he walked from his farm to the store carrying that milk and cream."

"Wasn't that about four miles or so?" They verify their recollections with one another.

"As a young man, he used to walk all the way from his farm up to town, in the morning, early, before sunup."

"And if you were out on that road as it was getting dark, there he would be, that'd be him walking home after work, after it was all over."

"He started out with a little hole in the wall, don't you know. He would parch peanuts, pop popcorn, make milkshakes, homemade ice cream, hot dogs, and hamburgers. He served them up in a little place with oilcloth tablecloths that he'd fixed up at the back of the store."

"I can still see him making those milkshakes," Ruby remembered. "You know in those days we didn't have any of those electric milkshake machines, so Daddy would put the milk and the ice cream and whatever flavoring somebody might want into a shaker and make them all by hand. On a hot day he might make three or four dozen or more."

"So, that's how he started. And that's how we started, too."

"I guess the people in Temple were a little like those people up there in West Virginia and Appalachia who didn't know they were poor until somebody went in there and told them they were. But we, unlike so many people then, continued to eat because we grew everything. We had vegetables and hogs, cows and milk and butter, eggs and chickens, and just about everything we needed."

"And with the store, we could get the other things, the things we couldn't grow."

"But there were a lot of people who weren't … who didn't have enough to eat. So while we certainly had to do without many times, we weren't as poor as some."

"We did own our own home, when many didn't. And we had the two farms, the little grocery store, and the restaurant. So much of that was due to our mother and daddy and their hard work, and the hard work of their families."

"And when we were little, we worked there with Daddy. We were always there, even as young girls."

"Oh yes. Even when we were just little young girls our little ol' daddy used to let us work behind the candy counter," Ruth recalled. "You know the kind they had back then, with the big thick glass and all that candy on display in it. You could go in and get ten of these for a penny and five of those for a penny. They'd go in a little paper sack, and you'd get a sackful of candy for ten or fifteen cents. Daddy always let us work the candy counter because we just loved it so much. And people would come in and buy candy from us when we were little girls there working in that store with our daddy."

"Daddy also let us roll up tobacco for folks. They'd come in and place their order and we loved to use that machine that rolled the cigarettes. We thought that was the greatest thing to take the tobacco and those little papers and run them through that machine that would seal them up. Then we'd put them in a little bag and give them to the customer."

"We started washing dishes before we started school."

"And we started school at five."

"We had all these chores to do. There wasn't anything Mama couldn't find for us to do."

"And she didn't let much time pass finding it, either."

"We'd pick up pine splinters and corn tops for kindling for the fireplace, gather stove wood and coal every evening."

"We'd water and feed the chickens and the cows and get water from the well."

"On Saturdays we'd sweep the yard to gather straw to make brush brooms and then we'd whitewash the trees with that lime concoction to keep the bugs down."

"On wash days we would fill the wash tubs."

"We had three of them; one for washing, one for rinsing, and one for bluing to make the white things white."

"And then of course we had to boil the clothes in this big old iron pot, so we had to get wood and get that going. There was that big iron pot bubbling away and three tubs working on washday and we were right there in the middle of it."

Ruby laughs as she recalls, "But I have always said that I thought the greatest invention that ever came along in our lives was the electric butter churn. Ruth and I just hated churning. I don't know why we hated it so much, but we did. And it would not do that one of us hit our churn one more lick than the other hit hers. So we'd count them out. I'd do fifty, then Ruth would do fifty. If one of us got fifty-one, then things just weren't right. Then as the butter got to forming, getting thicker, it would be thirty licks each, then twenty, and like that."

"And Mother was so meticulous about her butter. She would want all the moisture out of it and it had to be so smooth. She had a beautiful butter mold that she used, and she was just so particular about her butter that people would come from as far away as Atlanta to buy it."

"We hated that churning so much that we would spill the milk all over the place around the churn trying to get out of doing it."

"You know, trying to do a bad job so Mama wouldn't make us do it anymore."

"I don't know why," Ruby laughs, "but Mama never did fall for that, and we just kept on churning."

"We liked most every other chore Mama gave us, but churning and—"

"Picking bean weevils and potato bugs off the plants in the garden. That was just awful. We'd have to take a little can of kerosene out there with us and pick those bugs off and put them in that kerosene. If you'd ever done it, you'd understand. That and churning."

"When we grew older, we worked in the restaurant. We cooked, waited tables, washed dishes, and we made all the pastries, pies, and most everything—"

"For the store, all the pies, cakes, and desserts. We simply did all those things naturally. That was our life in those days. We never thought very much about it. We just did what we did and really did love, really loved every minute of it."

"Remember cutting up all those onions?" Ruby asked.

"Well, maybe not every minute," Ruth added, laughing.

Georgia in the 1930s, especially rural and small town Georgia as embodied by places like Temple, along with the rest of the nation, was hit hard by what became known as "The Great Depression." Things began to spiral out of control worldwide in 1928, but the devastating blow struck the United States on Black Tuesday, October 29, 1929, when the stock market crashed. The Crawford sisters were ten years old.

Georgia had not reached the Thirties in very good shape economically, and the Depression made things much worse. Already depressed crop prices, of special importance to any state dependent upon farming and agriculture, dropped precipitously by 50% or more, leading to the collapse of farming operations and the loss of family farmland and homes to the banks.

It is to the memories of people like Ruth and Ruby Crawford that the effects of the Depression on the rural and small-town South are consigned. They recall that there weren't soup kitchens, nor any other kind of help to speak of. Instead, neighbors depended upon neighbors. Rural and small-town families, many in and around Temple and places like it, were often displaced, unemployed, and broke. Photographs of the time from the cities chronicle able-bodied, unemployed men and their families standing in soup lines, an icon of the era. Rural America did not enjoy much assistance at all, nor very much in the way of public attention to draw notice to or to record the experiences of the ordeal.

"We were coming up, coming of age you might say, during the Depression," Ruth tells. "It taught us a lot of things. Things we haven't forgotten. We remember it well. Lots of things about it have stayed with us. Things like our friends and neighbors, and even people we didn't know very well in the community were doing without. Many were just devastated."

"Our little ol' daddy did whatever he could for folks like that," Ruby remembered. "I think that our watching him, seeing the way he helped people, well that might be why we decided when we were little girls that we wanted to help people to and we thought the best way to do that would be to grow up and become doctors. So for years that was our ambition."

"We remember all sorts of other things, like the fact that for a while there we didn't have an automobile. We didn't have a telephone. We didn't have … well who was it who had any money? Not a thing to spend to go anywhere."

"I mean a dollar was a dollar," Ruby reflected. "You know that little saying. Well, it really meant something then. And most people back then understood that."

"Hamburgers and hotdogs were about five cents apiece. A loaf of bread was a dime. Eggs were maybe ten cents a dozen. Those things like that could be had if someone had a little money or something to trade."

"People would bring all kinds of things to sell or trade. The farmers out in the rural areas would bring chickens to town to sell. So we had coops out back with a chicken-wire grill over the back to keep the chickens from getting out. They would swap the chickens for sugar, flour, coffee, and other necessities, things they had to have."

"Some people would bring eggs and sell them to Daddy, and then we'd sell the eggs to people who didn't have laying hens."

"But many times there wasn't anything to buy even if someone did have a little money."

"And sometimes there might be things to buy, but if no one had any cash, there might not be a way to buy it. So that's why people traded for things, work for food, or something they grew or made for something they needed."

"A dollar went about as far as it does today," they laugh, "which isn't very far."

"I guess we were poor, but we didn't know it," Ruth observed. "We worked hard, I can tell you that. But we had so much love in our family and were so happy that we never knew we were poor, if we were. We were more fortunate than many people, and we've never forgotten that either."

"Oh," Ruby remembered, "we used to have a big tank and pump, you know, so we could sell kerosene. There was a pump on the tank and we pumped it into those kerosene cans that people would bring to us, along with whatever they had to trade."

"A lot of people, including our family, had wood-burning stoves and used kerosene to start the fires. When we needed some we'd just go out there and pump a gallon or so."

"We had big hoop cheese, and when someone wanted a pound of cheese, you'd set the pressure, the cheese would come out, and you'd cut the cheese off that with a big shiny blade."

"We sold fish on Saturdays. Salt mackerel from a big barrel. They were saltwater fish and they came in a big wooden barrel and the fish were packed in there all covered with salt."

"People liked those salt mackerel because they were cheap and once you soaked them a little while in water or milk, if you had it, they weren't too bad."

"Our li'l ol' daddy could not stand to see anything go hungry," Ruth remembered. "I mean, if he was riding in the countryside and he'd see a cow or a horse that wasn't getting enough to eat, he'd get it something. We're living like that today, always have. We cannot stand to see anyone or anything going hungry. With all the food there is in this world, there's just no reason for it."

"He just couldn't stand to see another person go hungry, either," Ruby continued. "Merchants would come to town and poor farmers they'd need meat and milk, eggs, bread, and produce and didn't have any money. But he would still let them have whatever they needed."

"He had a big generous heart and he cared about people, especially if they didn't have enough to eat."

"We didn't have running water in those days, nor did we have electricity."

"We were about six years old before we got electricity."

"Before that, we used to have an icebox. We had a wooden icebox. The iceman would come by and we would hang a little card out that said that we wanted twenty-five, fifty, or a hundred pounds of ice, or more if we needed it. The milk and butter and other perishable foods were kept in that old wooden icebox."

"The ice went on the top, you know, because cold air settles. It sat in a metal pan that had a little hole in the back where the melt would drain off."

The sisters quizzed one another, "What was the first thing we got that was electric?"

"I know we didn't have a stove."

"I think the first electric thing we had might have been a refrigerator."

"Would it have been a refrigerator, the first electric thing?" they ask.

"I know we didn't have an electric stove for a long time," Ruth recalled, "because we cooked on a wood-burning stove. And we did that for a very long time."

"Radio?" they try to recall.

"A radio?"

"A radio. That must have been the first thing after the lights."

"Lights and then a radio. Most of the lights were just one-drop fixtures," Ruth gestured. "Just a piece of wire hanging down with the lightbulb attached to it. We had those for years, until we were able to buy nicer fixtures."

"On the radio we listened to the *Grand Ole Opry* from Nashville, Tennessee, with Uncle Dave Macon, Rodney and Boob Brasfield. George Hay, he called himself 'The Solemn Old Judge,' was the announcer. All those people who have long since gone to Heaven."

"Before we got our radio, though, our next door neighbor had a radio. On Saturday nights the whole neighborhood and all the nearby neighbors would congregate at his house and listen to the *Grand Ole Opry*."

"That was a regular Saturday night function."

Shortly after the girls started school, the *Grand Ole Opry* aired on October 18, 1925 under the title *Barn Dance*. Uncle Dave Macon, one of their favorites, appeared on the third broadcast and was a mainstay for years after that. In 1927, the show's name was changed to the *Grand Ole Opry*.

"Was there anything else we listened to?" Ruby wondered.

"Oh yes. We used to listen to the boxing matches. You could just imagine what was going on by listening to the announcers. They were so good it was just about like looking at it on television. It was fantastic."

"We were one of the first families in Temple to get a television set, but that was long years later."

"And then of course before television," Ruth recalled in an interview in the Atlanta PBS documentary *Lost Atlanta: The Way We Were*, "we loved WSB, you know. We used to listen to the *Farm and Home Hour* and wonderful Ernest Rogers and Lambdin Kay, who were quite a pair. And Charlie Smithgall–"

"And Bob Van Camp—"

"Hugh Ivey and Marcus Bartlett," Ruth continued, "who had the most melodious voice you'll ever hear on WSB, and who could play the piano wonderfully, too."

"The radio was the only electric thing we had in those days, and we loved every minute we listened to it."

"It was also at that time that we had lamps and you had to clean them, and put kerosene in them to burn. That was another of our chores Mama assigned us, washing lamp globes every Saturday."

"You wanted to be careful, because if your flame got too high, they'd get smoked up and have to be scrubbed clean."

"We studied by lamp."

"And sometimes by radio, but mostly by lamp."

WSB Radio went on the air on March 15, 1922, the same year the Lincoln Memorial opened to the public. WSB's first station manager, Lambdin Kay, became a pioneer in American radio by making WSB the first radio station in the country to have a slogan—The Voice of the South—and the first to employ a sound logo, three chimes, to signal its coming on the air, an innovation adopted throughout radio and later television. Known as "The Little Colonel" in the radio industry, Kay was the first in the country to recognize the educational power of the airwaves, and the station installed receiving equipment in schools around Atlanta, including local universities, Georgia Tech and Emory, and Agnes Scott College in Decatur, in its WSB's *University of the Air*.

"But even though we had a radio, we never went to bed without everyone gathering in front of the fireplace, all of us, and Daddy would read some verses from the Bible and we would all say our prayers, and then we'd go to bed. We did that all our lives."

In 1931, when Ruth and Ruby were barely teenagers, thirty-three year old Richard B. Russell, Jr., one of thirteen children from Winder, Georgia, was sworn into office as Governor of the State of Georgia. It was around that time that the Crawford girls began to become aware politically. Eugene Talmadge made his first run for governor in 1932 and would be elected then and again in 1934, 1940, and 1946. Talmadge was a fascinating though polarizing figure in Georgia politics. In the elections during the 1930s, rural counties provided much of Talmadge's support, while urban counties consistently opposed him.

It was in Temple that the Crawford sisters first heard Talmadge, a master campaigner from "the stump," and began their life-long interest in politics. Talmadge's campaign slogan resounded with people all over the state who were living through the same and often worse circumstances as the Crawford family. He spoke to them and theirs by telling them that, "The poor dirt farmer ain't got but three friends on this earth: God Almighty, Sears Roebuck, and Gene Talmadge." Hearing that, Ruth and Ruby were bitten by the political bug and enjoyed the ailment from then on.

Franklin Roosevelt was in the White House, and the country was limping through recovery with the alphabet soup that was the WPA (Works Projects Administration), the CCC (Civilian Conservation Corps), the TVA (Tennessee Valley Authority), the SEC (Securities and Exchange Commission), and the FDIC (Federal Deposit Insurance Corporation).

In 1936, when Ruth and Ruby were in their teens, Margaret Mitchell published probably the single most famous piece of literature about Atlanta that the world has ever known, surpassing and outlasting the fame that a later Olympic bid would bring to the city. Hitting the shelves with little or no publicity, *Gone With the Wind* was not an instant bestseller. But that would soon change when David O. Selznick paid $50,000 for the movie rights, the highest figure at the time ever paid for a first novel. The book won the 1937 Pulitzer Prize, and in 1939, people all over Georgia nearly swooned when the movie premiered at the Loew's Grand Theater in Atlanta, attracting many of the film's stars to that gala event and the parade that preceded it.

While Margaret Mitchell was writing *Gone With the Wind*, she and her husband John Marsh lived in an old house in Atlanta at 979 Crescent Avenue that had been converted into apartments some years before. It was the place Margaret Mitchell later called "The Dump." In fact, it was a literary salon of sorts, quite popular in the late 20s and early 30s when Mitchell and Marsh lived there, modeled as it was on the French salons of the Enlightenment and the more modern Algonquin Roundtable made famous by Dorothy Parker and friends. In 1994, after attempts by arsonists to do away with the place, actions many suspected were prompted by developers with designs on that most valuable piece of downtown Atlanta real estate, "The Dump" was restored by Daimler–Benz in time for the 1996 Summer Olympics. Today it houses The Center for Southern Literature and is officially known as "The Margaret Mitchell House."

"I can remember," Ruby recalled, "coming to Atlanta, in December, and waiting on the sidewalk for four hours in the cold just to catch a glimpse of Clark Gable. Ruth and I stood across the street from the First National Bank of Atlanta building, having no idea in the world that we would be working there in a few years, and for thirty-three years after that."

"They had a parade the day of the premier at Loew's Grand Theater. We didn't have an invitation to the premier or the ball they had that night, but we got to see all the stars—Clark Gable, Vivien Leigh, Leslie Howard who played Ashley Wilkes, Butterfly McQueen who played Prissy, Anne Rutherford, and all those others. We were so excited."

"We didn't get to go to the movie that night, but it wasn't long before we were back and seeing it many times. It's our favorite movie of all time. We think it's the best movie ever made and we watched it every chance we had."

"And who would have known when we were standing on that street corner waiting all that time that in a few years we would be working in the bank and having breakfast at Jacob's Pharmacy right there in the bank building with Margaret Mitchell. She came in there all the time in those days and we got to know her."

Chapter Three

A Simple Matter of Physics

Genius is one percent inspiration,
ninety-nine percent perspiration.
—Thomas Alva Edison

In developing his theories of relativity, Einstein contemplated energy. Newton pondered gravity in his *Principia*. Galileo in *De Motu* studied motion. None was able to consider Ruth and Ruby Crawford. Had any been able to, rethinking of theories might have been necessary. Contemplating irresistible forces and immovable objects has occupied and intrigued mankind for centuries. But who would ever have reckoned that li'l ol' tow-headed twin sisters from a hamlet in the American South who were reared in the Roaring Twenties, came of age during the Great Depression, and matured in wartime, would, or could, with their feet planted firmly on the Earth, take on an industry, a city, and in fact, a nation, doing so with an elan and aplomb every bit as refined as their minds are sharp? Above all, none—not the industry, not the city, nor the nation—contemplated being overmatched.

—

Horse sense is that sense
that a jackass doesn't have.

But where did this begin? How did it start? What honed those minds?

"We started school at Temple Elementary School," remembered Ruth.

"That was our school through seventh grade," Ruby added.

"Then high school was freshman, sophomore, junior, and senior–four years at that time. Eleven years of school."

"We turned sixteen a little before we graduated. But we were fifteen almost all the year we were seniors."

"It was wonderful growing up in a small town. We had fine schools. We had the best teachers. We got as good as or maybe even better an education in Temple than we would have in any of the Atlanta schools. Our teachers were strict and they demanded that we study."

"We had courses like algebra and geometry, and not just the basics, but the advanced courses, too. I still haven't figured out how geometry has helped me," Ruby observed, "but I'm working on it."

"We had three years of Latin, which helped us later on in law school."

"Those teachers demanded the best, and they didn't let anyone get by with anything. We should go back to those days of teaching grammar and math and history and all the subjects they taught us that people don't seem to know a thing about any more."

While in high school, Ruth and Ruby also got jobs as switchboard operators for the telephone company in Temple. "The telephone operator was a friend of ours, so she would let us come work the switchboards. We worked at the phone company—"

"For a dollar a day," Ruby remembers. "That was big money in Temple, Georgia, at that time."

"And at Daddy's store, we worked there, too."

"And in the restaurant."

"And then we wrote news for the newspaper."

"It was a dollar a column," Ruby recalled of their working for three newspapers: *The Villa Rica Breeze, The Bremen Gateway,* and *The Tallapoosa Journal.* "Now that was really big money in those days. We covered everything from national news, to state events, politics, sports, society. You name it. We wrote it."

"All kinds of things–high school football games, marriages, bridge parties, the social news, and even obituaries. Anything that happened, we wrote about it."

—

Footprints in the sands of time
are not made by people wearing loafers.

"We were always busy. Daddy had the grocery store and the restaurants, he had acquired another one somewhere along the line, and we had the farms, one from our mother's family, and Daddy's farm. We weren't farmers as such, but Daddy was a master gardener and grew everything under the sun. We were at home nearly every weekend, always picking something, shelling something, freezing or canning something. We've been doing that all our lives, too."

In his poem "To A Mouse," Robert Burns, upon seeing a mouse's nest upturned by a plow, observes that "the best laid schemes of mice and men oft go astray." Similarly, external forces over which they had no control, a depression, a world war, and the political and cultural setting of the time, all acted on the plans of Ruth and Ruby Crawford. Coming to Atlanta with plans to enter the medical profession, something few women did in 1943, the Crawford sisters came face to face with the unpleasant reality that there was simply not enough money for both of them to go to medical school.

Ruby recalled, that "In those days there were no HOPE Scholarships, nor much, if any, student aid available."

The sisters stated emphatically, "We wanted to be doctors." In explaining their motivation, each maintained, "We like helping people. Whatever we did, we wanted to do some good. If we couldn't, we weren't interested in doing whatever it was." Ruth and Ruby, individually or together, will tell anyone listening that they firmly believe, "The Lord had other plans for us."

Ruby does say that, "We have always regretted that we weren't able to go to medical school. We thought when we came to Atlanta that we'd work a few years and save some money and be able to go. But it didn't work out like that. We had that ambition from the time we were very young. We used to play doctor all the time when we were girls. That ambition stayed with us until we got into the banking classes and began to like law, and we realized we could become lawyers. That's when our ambition changed. But before that it was always going to medical school and becoming doctors."

"On January 18, 1943," Ruth recounted, "we started working at the First National Bank of Atlanta."

The First National Bank of Atlanta later became known as First Atlanta. It succeeded the Atlanta National Bank, federally chartered in September 1865 as the first bank in Atlanta to receive a charter after the Civil War. That bank, now Wachovia, represents the longest continuously operating bank in the city.

In 1916, Atlanta National Bank bought and merged with American National Bank, also in Atlanta, and then in 1924 the two merged with Lowry Bank and Trust to become Atlanta and Lowry National Bank. A 1929 merger with the Fourth National Bank formed the First National Bank of Atlanta, then the largest bank in the country south of Philadelphia. For many years, throughout the 1940s and well into the 1970s, the First National Bank of Atlanta held the distinction of being, as measured by its deposits, the largest commercial bank in the Southeast.

By 1943, Atlanta had become the banking center of the Southeastern United States largely because the Federal Reserve had in 1914 chosen Atlanta as the site for a new Federal Reserve Bank. Politics and economics of the time dictated that the country could no longer operate with a central bank located only in the Northeast. In response, twelve banks were opened throughout the United States, including one in the South. The bank in Atlanta was, much like Federal Reserve Banks in other areas of the country, unique to its region. That is, the bank was run by Southerners, whose fortunes were dependent upon agriculture and the money still to be made from cotton. While resistence lingered in the South to anything "federal," the Federal Reserve Bank stabilized and developed standards for banking throughout the region, contributing to the proliferation of banks in and around Atlanta and the region.

When the Federal Reserve Bank came to Atlanta, New Orleans was the financial center of the South. Atlanta's location and its railway operations, along with the Bank, changed all that for good and propelled Atlanta past every other Southern city, many of which were port cities like Savannah, Wilmington, Charleston, and Jacksonville. Understandably, there was a great deal of discontent in cities that were passed over. In New Orleans, residents held a mass rally protesting Atlanta's having been chosen as the site for the new federal bank. Despite the protest, the Bank's first home became the then-new Hurt Building in downtown Atlanta, a structure that still stands today and which for many years housed the headquarters of the State Bar of Georgia.

"We thought maybe we'd try to get a civil service job because we thought they paid so well."

"But Mr. Elbert Reeves," Ruth explained, "who was with Jefferson Standard Life Insurance Company, used to come to Temple. He would eat in our restaurant, and he thought we were wasting our time out in little bitty ol' Temple. He thought we ought to be in Atlanta, and he knew we wanted to get an education. So he, himself, called his friend, Freeman Strickland, one of the vice-presidents over at First National Bank of Atlanta, and he also called his friend at C & S Bank and had them mail us applications."

"Mr. Reeves had also called Southern Bell and had them send us applications."

"We were thinking at the time that maybe we could go into the civil service and have a government job, so we filled out the applications, but we didn't come over to Atlanta for an interview. Our plan was that we would work at whatever jobs we got and save money so we could go to medical school. We had no idea then that things would work out the way they did and that we would spend the next thirty-three years doing what we did."

"Then on January 2nd, the day after New Year's Day, the telephone rang in our father's store and we answered it, and it was one of the vice-presidents of the First National Bank of Atlanta saying that they had read the applications and while they usually did not employ relatives–they did not do that in those days—they would make an exception in our case if we would be willing to come to work for them. They wanted to talk to both of us."

"They wanted us both to come in for an interview," Ruby echoed. "We thought that was just wonderful."

"So we thought well maybe we would get a job at the bank and then maybe later on we might transfer over to Southern Bell."

"They most likely would have given us jobs as long-distance operators or in accounting."

"But when the bank offered us just a little bit more money, we started there. Ruth had always played banker anyway, when we were young girls, so it was a good fit."

"When we weren't playing doctor, I would go with Daddy whenever he went to the bank. When I went with him, I was the banker. And Ruby, well, she was the postmaster."

"Yes," Ruby says proudly, "I was the postmaster, and she was the banker."

"Oh me," the sisters laughed, recalling how important they were by holding such high offices at such tender years.

Ruth recalled, "Our first job with the bank was in the Bookkeeping Department. That's not where we thought we were going to start out. We thought they were going to make us switchboard operators. But they didn't. They put us in the Bookkeeping Department. I just loved it. We had the greatest boss and the most fun, and I just loved our old Burroughs bookkeeping machines and posting all those checks and deposits."

A lifetime of training, eagerness to learn, and attention to detail began to pay dividends for them very soon after the Crawford sisters were hired. Ruby tells it this way: "When we went to the bank we heard that the best jobs in the bank were in the Trust Department. But you had to be really good, and in favor with some of the hierarchy, to get into the Trust Department."

"Before I had been there a year, I got a call from Mr. Adamson, who was the vice-president in charge of personnel. Everybody just feared him. People thought he was like a big bear and they were scared to death of him. He was from Carroll County where we were from, and maybe we got off on the right foot with him by being from Carroll. He sent for me one day and I thought, 'Oh, my goodness what in the world have I done?' I thought I was going to be fired. But when I got to his desk he had all these lovely things to say about me! He told me that they had been observing my work and that they were very impressed. He said that they wanted to put me in a position where I would be able to progress faster in the bank and make a little more money and all that sort of thing and that they had an opening in the Trust Department! I thought, 'My Lord, it would be forty years before I ever got in there.' So they made me manager of the Real Estate Division over taxes and insurance and escrows, and that was my first job in the Trust Department. That was before I had been there a year."

"'43 or '44?" Ruth asked.

"The latter part of '43."

"Mr. Adamson," Ruth reported, "was also the one who said that the only regret he had in hiring us was that we weren't sextuplets. He said he wished he had four more just like us. And when Ruby went to the Trust Department, I went downstairs to be a savings teller. That was a step up for me, too. Neither one of us wanted to leave the Bookkeeping Department. We had such a great time there—we had the greatest group of people and our boss—"

"Never had one better, any place, any time, than we did there. And we just loved him to death. We just had the greatest group of girls, and we had more fun. We just couldn't wait to get up and go to work every morning."

"His name was W. V. Austin."

"William V. Austin was just the greatest boss. And then there was Wilbur Cohen who was the assistant manager of the Bookkeeping Department, and he was so much fun. Wilbur Cohen and William V. Austin, they were two of the greatest."

"So I was in the Trust Department in 1943 and Ruth was in the Savings Department."

"That's right. We took care of savings accounts only. In those days things were divided into departments. If you put money in a savings account, you went to the Savings Department. If you wanted commercial banking, you went to Commercial. I was still in the Savings Department one day when the auditor of the bank wanted to talk to me."

"So, like Ruby, I was pretty nervous, wondering what I had done. But, anyway, he offered me a job in the Accounting Department, or Auditing, as they termed it. That's how I wound up going to Auditing. That's where you started in Accounting. And when I said I would do that, everything worked out for the positive."

Banking, like most of American business and industry, has traditionally been dominated by men. Until the early 1940s, banking had been almost totally a man's world, an industry where men had a decided edge in hiring, longevity, promotions, and exclusive access to the upper levels of management and to boards of directors. There were really two issues confronting most women: positions and pay, coupled of course with prejudice, posturing, and parsimony. Shortly before Ruth and Ruby moved to Atlanta, women were expected to be content to be tellers, switchboard operators, typists, receptionists, or secretaries. There was little opportunity for advancement, and what did come, came hard. Women were not often found forming the ranks of supervisors, department heads, managers, or officers, and it would have been extremely unusual to find a woman in a boardroom anywhere in America, and most especially in the Southeast. In truth, and for quite a long time after the Crawford sisters were hired by the bank, such a thing was simply unheard of.

The Crawford sisters will be the first to admit that, although they worked hard, their lives were certainly not all work and no play. They enjoyed all manner of things, and despite their professional demands, they pursued their education while living basically in two places most weeks—Atlanta and Temple.

"As for our social lives, we never gave up anything," Ruby remembers. "Some people sacrifice everything, but we didn't. We dated a lot and went out a lot at night."

"When we were younger it was nearly impossible to tell us apart, and we so loved being twins. We also liked to have a little fun with it."

"Once when we were teenagers, I sent Ruth out on a date with a fellow I had been dating. I liked that boy well enough and we had a date all set up, but then this other boy asked me out. I was so in love with him. Oh my! He was my first love. So I had Ruth go out with the first boy, and he never knew the difference."

"Another time we were double dating and our dates wanted to stop off at the hospital to see a friend of theirs who was sick. We waited in the car for them, and while they were gone we decided that it would be great fun to switch places for the rest of the evening. They couldn't tell us apart either."

"But we later fessed up to that one."

—

I just want a platonic relationship
–play for him, tonic for me.

"We went to the All-Star Concert series. We had season tickets. We loved music and plays. Oh, and we went to wrestling matches on Saturdays."

"We'd have opera one night and wrestling matches the next night. We loved baseball and went to ball games all the time."

"We never have been known for the amount of sleep we get," Ruth added.

"Atlanta had a lot of nice movie theaters, and we had streetcars to get around. There wasn't as much to do as there is now with all the entertainment, but we could go down to the old City Auditorium and they'd have music."

"There were two other sets of twins named Ruth and Ruby and we all went on the same night, so there were three sets of Ruths and Rubys out in Atlanta at one time. Ruth and Ruby Webb worked at Life of Georgia Insurance Company as executive secretaries to Howard Dobbs and Cody Laird. The other two were Ruth and Ruby Cowan. They, the Cowans, worked at separate places and didn't dress alike every day, but they were at the concerts, and people used to marvel at three sets of twins. We sat very close together," Ruby recalled, "The other four have since passed away."

"We shopped at Rich's. They had the Great Tree at Rich's and they would light it at Thanksgiving. We would get out and walk around down there at Five Points. That was the Wall Street of Atlanta. All the banks were there. It was the financial center of the city. I regret that it ever started moving out, because it was great. You could walk on the streets and speak to people. You knew a lot of people. Ruby and I were involved in so many things after we started at the bank. We were involved in the Women Accountants group, and the Chamber of Commerce, and later the Georgia Association for Women Lawyers and the Atlanta Bar Association and so many things like that. In those days, you could just walk down the street and you knew everyone."

"I had a guest come into town one time and we went out to lunch," Ruby related, "and he said, 'Do you know everyone in the city of Atlanta?' and I said,

'No,' and he said, 'Well, you speak to everyone in the street.' But everyone did that. Between going to school and working and socializing, we knew people. Having had newspaper experience, we wound up being editors of the First National Bank bulletin. So we met a lot of people that way, too."

Ruth recalled, "When we started in January of 1943 we were enrolled immediately in the Draughon's School of Commerce and also the American Institute of Banking. We were in banking school to earn our certificates in banking within two weeks after we started to work at the bank."

"Draughon's was where we went to learn bookkeeping, accounting, secretarial skills, typing, shorthand, and anything else needed in a business office," Ruby added.

"At the time, it was the largest business school in the state. So many people went there."

"While we went to school there, we were also enrolled in banking school at the American Institute of Banking."

"The whole experience, Draughon's and the AIB school, was like grammar school, high school, and college all in one."

"The AIB was the largest educational institution of its kind in the world. That's where we eventually earned our certificates in banking."

"We had to have a lot of course work, commercial law, negotiable instruments, contracts, trusts, and classes like that. That's when we became interested in law. We loved our teacher, J. Pollard Turman; he was just our greatest mentor in life. He was just a wonderful lawyer, and we loved him to death."

"J. Pollard Turman was counsel for the Federal Reserve Bank. He later became President of the Bank, and then he headed the J. M. Tull Corporation. He was the man who had more influence on us, more confidence in us, and who helped us as much as anyone. I really do think he was our greatest mentor," Ruby agreed.

"After we had been at the bank a little while," Ruth remembered, "we figured out that there wasn't going to be enough money for both of us to go to medical school."

"And you know," Ruby recalls, "I thought, this law is so interesting, maybe we could go to law school at night, since we can't go to medical school."

"That's when we decided to go to law school."

"Of course, even if we had saved the money for both of us to go to school to become doctors, we would have had to wait for a few years, because at the time Emory didn't admit women into its medical school. So we went to law school," Ruby said matter-of-factly.

"Once we had taken the law courses and became interested in law it was just a matter of time. I don't remember exactly how long it was before we started, but I would have to guess we started law school in '45 or '46. We got our Masters Degrees in law in '49. We were admitted to practice in '48. We were at Georgia State and went there for tax work after we were admitted to practice. We did most of the tax work after we got out of law school and we also took Accounting 1 and 2, Economics 1 and 2, Principles of Banking, Investment, Public Relations, and Trusts, subjects that we had already taken in banking school. But we had to have them to get our degrees."

"We enrolled in Atlanta Law School. Classes were at night. The school was run by Dean Hamilton Douglas. He was assisted by Judge Herschel Cole. Judge Cole was the most wonderful man. We just loved him. He was a great teacher, a good judge, and a delightful man."

"We just had the best time going through law school. We loved our course work and our classmates and our teachers."

Atlanta Law School no longer exists, having closed in the mid–1990s. It was one of three night law schools that operated in Atlanta from the 1930s through 2004. A significant number of judges, prosecutors, and private attorneys obtained their legal education at Atlanta or at the other two night law schools, Woodrow Wilson School of Law, which closed in the 1980s, and John Marshall School of Law that continues to operate. The purpose of the night law schools was to meet the needs of people just like the Crawford sisters, that is, people who worked full time and who had no other way to obtain a legal education except by attending evening classes.

"In 1948 we took the exam and were admitted to the Georgia Bar."

"We never practiced privately. Well, except one time, when Ruby had a good friend going through a divorce. Her husband didn't want to pay anything and she didn't have a lot of money to pay for lawyers to fight him. But she did need some help. And Ruby helped her."

"I got her a very good settlement, I must say. I don't think her husband thought very much of this lady lawyer, his wife's friend, who was helping her out. I don't know what he took me for, but she ended up with a lot more than he ever wanted to give up."

"Except for that, we practiced for our employer, for the bank."

—

You may be on the right track
but you're liable to get run over
if you just sit there.

Just when it might seem that working full time, finding a place to live, commuting home to Temple on the weekends, and maintaining a social life in Atlanta and a church life in Temple was "a gracious plenty," the Crawford sisters met and cleared another educational and professional hurdle. They obtained Masters of Law degrees, and then began taking college business and accounting courses at Georgia State University. While the Crawford sisters were doing all this, they also began to move up in the bank hierarchy, at least to the level customary at the time.

In the rare instances where a woman was able to move into a supervisory or management capacity, it was good business for the bank. The reason was very simple; the bank could and did receive more work for less money. Base salaries were nowhere near the level men enjoyed and raises were often either non-existent or fractions of what men at the same rank received.

"The man at the next desk might get a hundred-dollar raise," Ruth recalled, "where we'd get five."

"If we were lucky."

"We did more work than they did, but we sure weren't paid the same."

"Our daddy kept telling us, 'Get on out of there. They're not going to do anything for you.'"

"We stayed because we thought we could make a difference," they agree. "We thought it would change."

Chapter Four

Southern Belles and Streetcars

We believe in moonlight, magnolias, and mint juleps
… We believe in dressing up.
— Ruth and Ruby Crawford

That these two sisters, and in pretty short order, became lawyers, accountants, educators, writers, and speakers while working demanding full-time jobs is remarkable enough. But to do so in jobs that few women held, in a business barely penetrated by women beyond a teller's cage, a switchboard, or the secretarial pool, and to turn in one accomplishment after another, meeting and exceeding challenge after challenge, all while working actively in more civic causes than can easily be counted, entertaining, traveling, and remaining very active in the life of their church, has the potential to tire even the most casual observer.

Clearly, Ruth and Ruby have generated a lot of press over the years. Much of it is professional in nature, noting a career advancement, a promotion, or an outstanding performance turned in by one or the other or both ladies. But an equal or perhaps greater share of the gallons of ink devoted to the Crawford sisters has been devoted to recognizing and keeping track of their community contributions, stewardship, and the civic responsibilities they have assumed.

Many who have written about Ruth and Ruby have employed the image of the Southern belle in their descriptions of the sisters. They have done so with the sisters' endorsement. Both ladies are quite proud of being Southern, and prouder still of being women. That they are accomplished women is all the better.

Ruth and Ruby are the subjects of a chapter in Maryln Schwartz's book *A Southern Belle Primer, or Why Princess Margaret Will Never Be A Kappa Kappa Gamma*. In her wickedly accurate compilation of things Southern and belle-ish, Ms. Schwartz presents the twins with the same balance that they have maintained in their lives since girlhood:

"Ruth and Ruby are twins and a pair of Atlanta belles who were carefully taught by their mother that there is tacky and then

there is tacky tacky ... 'We believe in moonlight, magnolias, and mint juleps ... We believe in dressing up.'

The twins say they delight in being feminine and are firm on one thing. They just don't believe a lady ever has to tell her age. 'Age is immaterial ...' But don't ever think these Southern ladies do nothing but loll under magnolia[s] ... all day. [A] friend explains [that] 'those are the most energetic ladies I have ever seen ... they are ladies in the true Southern belle fashion: they look like cream puffs and get things done like Sherman tanks.'" pp.25-26

—

Age is just a number and mine is unlisted.

Many times over the years the sister have been asked, perhaps by those who have not read Emily Post's etiquette manual, about their age. Ruth recalled that many times when the sisters would meet someone, they were often asked, "How old are you guys?"

Her response was, "Now what difference does that make? Age doesn't mean anything to us. We just keep doing what we're doing."

Ruby defuses such indelicate inquiries with humor. Among her many responses to the age question, Ruby will dispense with a smile and a twinkle, "I'm old enough to know the score and young enough to play the game," or "I'm young enough to have a future and old enough to have a past," or "I'm old enough to light your flame and young enough to keep it burning."

While complimentary and always used with the best of intentions, the label "Southern belle" hardly tells the whole story of Ruth and Ruby. Clearly, these women take pride in who and what they are. They do so graciously, while preserving and celebrating their femininity. But, and this is important, they are much more than Southern belles.

The American Heritage Dictionary defines "belle" as, "A popular, attractive girl or woman, especially the most attractive one of a group." Southern we know, and the ladies have always been popular and attractive. Their colorful matching outfits have been a trademark since their mother began sewing for them when they were very young, as were at one time the twin Cadillacs they owned and their dear twin poodles, Kandi and Kisses. In the time they were involved most heavily with their careers with the bank, they were among the most gracious and active entertainers in the busy and growing city of Atlanta.

Not surprisingly, and with no disrespect intended to any Southern belle or any fan of any Southern belle, the term "belle" when applied to Ruth and Ruby Crawford begins to unravel and fall a little short, eventually becoming wholly inadequate when considered against the prodigious amount of work and service these women accomplished in their lives. Much of it, most especially the professional and civic achievements, is not generally characteristic of those thought of as belles, Southern or otherwise. That does not mean that Ruth and Ruby are averse to the term or to being thought of in that way. The point is that the label "Southern belle" when used to describe the Crawford sisters, simply must be content to elbow its way onto the long list of other words that describe these "two little ol' tow-head twin girls from Temple, Georgia."

The sisters agree that in none of their pursuits has it been "necessary to sacrifice our femininity."

By all accounts they have not.

—

A man opens a door for a lady
not because she is a lady,
but because he is a gentleman.

From the time it became the state capital, Atlanta began to expand. Neighborhoods that are famous now, Inman Park, North Druid Hills, Morningside, Ansley Park, and others, began to take root. Downtown, great surges in building took place, tracks for trolleys were laid, and wires to power them were erected overhead. It was a common thing for the Crawford girls to visit the city from the time they were very young. It was a place that excited and amazed them. But when they arrived in January of 1943, they were in Atlanta as young women, without family to accompany them, and a long, though not unmanageable, forty-five miles from Temple.

"What was Atlanta like in 1943?" the ladies asked one another.

"Well, let's see. There were only about 300,000 people, maybe a little more," Ruby recounted. "In the whole area. Not just in the city."

"And Ruby and I saw most of the big buildings go up in Atlanta. We had street cars, right there at Five Points …"

"Ten cents a ride."

"Ten cents a ride, finally went up to fifteen cents, I think. In fact, Ruby and I rode the street car to work from Fairview Road, right around the corner from our place on Oakdale Road, over near Brightwood and Springdale Parks."

In the television production *Lost Atlanta: The Way We Were*, produced by Georgia Public Television in 1994 and aired in 1999 and 2001, Ruth recalled, "We just loved the trolleys. In fact, when we came to Atlanta as children, we can still remember ... the noise of the streetcars. We were so intrigued by that. We can also remember the horses' hooves, and the horse-drawn carriages and wagons ... that they used to haul ice and coal ... in those days. I can still hear the sounds of those hooves on the pavement. But we loved the 'clang, clang, clang of the trolley.'"

It is said by those who recall that individual streetcar drivers could be recognized by the "tunes" they played on their trolley bells as they plied their way from outlying towns like Decatur and Marietta into and through the crowded streets of old downtown Atlanta.

During World War II, the city's streetcars began to be converted to "trackless trolleys," that is, electrically-powered buses. The last real streetcar ran in Atlanta on April 10, 1949. Suburban development, bigger highways, and an increased number of multi-car families put the trackless trolleys out of business in the early 1960s, relegating them and the old streetcars to sidings and static displays of the way things had once been. Interestingly, and perhaps not surprisingly given Atlanta's fond memories of her streetcars and the ever-increasing burdens of traffic in the area, in 2007 a group known as Atlanta Streetcar, Inc. was formed with the goal of bringing streetcars back to the city. The organization's "goal is to create a modern streetcar line," much like what Atlanta had in the 30s and 40s.

"Our friend Clark Harrison used to drive through to work on Fairview Road to miss Ponce de Leon traffic, and he'd give us a ride."

"A lot of times our friend, Mr. James Malone, would come along at the streetcar stop and he'd pick us up. As did Mr. Donald Hastings. Back then you'd pick people up if their car was stopped, or if they needed a ride. We could trust those people."

"Sometimes we'd be going to school late at night and we'd get off the streetcar and walk home in the dark and thought nothing of it."

Ruby remembers, "When we came over to Atlanta and interviewed with Mr. Lester who was in charge of personnel at the bank, he told Ruth and me how important it was to have a good address in Atlanta, which we knew to be true. So instead of finding some cheap place to live, we looked in the nice part of Piedmont Avenue, but we didn't find anything. So we went to Druid Hills to begin with and lived on Fairview Road, which runs into Lullwater. One of our directors at the bank lived on Fairview, too."

"Mr. Malone. He headed Retail Credit. So we lived there, and then we went to Oakdale Road for twenty-five years before we moved to Buckhead."

"We had a nice place when we first got here, in a rooming house. It was enough for us then."

"But it didn't take us long to outgrow it," Ruth remembered.

"It's still there. It was one of our biggest mistakes not trying to buy it."

For many years Ruth and Ruby led double lives. Weekdays were devoted to working in Atlanta at the bank, going to school at night, and carrying on some of the social life in which young ladies engaged at that time. The weekends saw them in Temple with their family and in the community where they had grown up, doing the things they had done all their lives.

"In those days, we were active in our church in Atlanta, but nowhere near like we would be later on. Mostly we went to our church at home in Temple because we went to Temple every weekend on Friday and came back Monday morning after breakfast."

"Daddy always wanted us to stay as long as possible."

"Sometimes," Ruth recalled, "when we were leaving early on a Monday morning, he'd say, 'Oh honey, it's so long until Friday.'"

"In Temple we did everything. We worked in the garden, mowed the lawn, cooked, raised flowers, and went to our home church."

"We did a lot of social work in the church, washed all the cars at home, did work for Mother and Daddy, helped garden, tend, pick, shell, and freeze just about any vegetable you can name. We did all those things on weekends."

"We picked and arranged flowers for every room in the house," Ruth reminisced. "We had a big flower garden and did all that was necessary to keep it up. We had a lot of roses."

"We had about seventy-five rose bushes," Ruby added. "And we used to fix flowers and take them to people. We'd arrange flowers for every room in the house, the kitchen, dining room, patio, and for the church on the third Sunday of every month for about thirty years."

"We also built a sixteen-hundred brick patio."

"Just the two of us."

"I've never been so sore in my life," Ruth recalled. "We could hardly move when we got back to Atlanta that Monday morning. It was all I could do to drive to Atlanta that day."

"When I first woke up, I was afraid I would die, but the next morning I was afraid I wouldn't die. When I got to my office," Ruby laughs, "I told the people in my office that if they wanted anything from me that day they should say so right then, because once I sat down, I wouldn't be able to get up. It took us until Thursday or Friday to limber up."

"Ruby and I just did too much in one weekend, stooping over that many times, picking up sixteen hundred bricks. Laying that many bricks was just beyond comprehension. We should have done it in two or three weekends, or maybe four, instead of one. We've never been as near dead in our lives."

"But that patio was so pretty, and we were so proud of it, but we just never should have tried it the way we did…"

"Oh, how Mother and Daddy and all of us enjoyed that patio. We even had a flower bed. It was about a foot and a half wide all around the patio. It was a space that we built especially for flowers."

"And we had an umbrella table and a grill, and we'd cook out every weekend. Daddy loved that."

"A young man from Temple who was in the 4-H Club had to do a project, so he came down to see our brick patio because he wanted to do one just like it."

"When he got there to see the patio, he said he didn't know how we had time to do it."

"We were happy that he wanted to build a patio like ours, but we warned him not to try to do it all in one weekend."

"I don't remember where we learned to lay bricks," Ruth said. "But when we were girls we were in the 4-H club for years and learned to do a lot of things, cooking, making our own clothes, dresses, pajamas, and blouses."

"I remember after that we always did our own sewing."

"Our mother had previously done it for us," Ruth recalled. "She made us beautiful clothes with smocking and embroidery and lace and shirring, and she had to make two of everything. Ladies had time to sew in those days, but now if something happens and I rip a seam or lose a button, I have to go out and buy a new outfit because I don't have time to sew a stitch or even a button on."

"We were out there in Temple one Saturday, and Daddy had this pickup truck, and Ruth and I just loved that pickup. We'd park that Cadillac and get in the pickup truck and just have a ball. He bought the truck from a neighbor who had to sell it because his daughter got married and she couldn't afford a car, so he was going to buy her a car. So he said to Daddy, 'Don't you want to buy the pickup truck?' Daddy said, 'Yes, I'll buy it.' Ruth and I loved it. We just loved putting on our jeans, real blue jeans—"

"And our red plaid shirts—"

"And driving all over Temple, taking turns at the wheel."

"One Saturday," Ruth remembered, "A man called down to the house and wanted to know if Daddy was there. We said he wasn't, and he said, 'Oh, I was just wondering if Mr. Crawford would haul a load of wood for me in his truck.' Well, Daddy was working, filling in for a man who had a grocery store and flea market who was sick that day. So he asked Daddy to come help out. We told the man on the phone that Daddy was working, but that we would do it. We heard this pause, like he thought, 'I'll bet you will.' And we said we would be there in a few minutes."

"We had on our jeans and our red plaid shirts, and we took our two little dogs with us."

"There were all these slabs of cord wood. We got out there to load that truck and the man said, 'Oh, ladies, I'll load that,' and we said, 'No, we're here to help you.' So we loaded that pickup truck with all that wood. When we went to deliver it, of course we had to get it off. The first load was to the home of the lady whose daughter had worked for us. That man saw us driving up in that pickup truck and he must have been thinking he was going to have to unload that truck. But we got it all off and we started back toward his house and he said, 'Let's go to the house and have a bite of lunch. My wife will expect you all to eat with us.'"

"We said, 'No, thank you, we just had breakfast, so we'll eat a little later on.' He told us, 'But I'd like to haul another load if you all have time.' So we said, 'Oh, don't worry about us.' Well, we loaded up the truck again, and he was just so flabbergasted that we had that truck all loaded as soon as we did."

"Next door to that man's house, this neighbor had a cotton gin and sold coal, cord wood, and other things," Ruth recalled, "and he was the Baptist preacher there in town. He looked out and saw us loading that truck and he walked over said, 'Oh, my goodness, I wish that Ed Smith could see you now.' Well, Ed Smith was the President of our bank. We said, 'I wish he could, too. We'd ask him to come over here and help us load this truck.' He said, 'Well ladies, when you get this load delivered, I've got some coal I want you to haul.'"

"So we said, 'We'll be back.'"

"I think they offered us a dollar a load but we said, 'Just forget about that. We're glad to do it. Daddy would have done it for you.' So they thought we were so nice to haul that wood for him that day."

"Daddy asked later," Ruby added, 'Did he try to pay you?' And we said, 'Yes, he tried to give us a dollar but we wouldn't take it, of course.' We told Daddy we'd rather work for free than have people think we would work that cheap."

Chapter Five

The War Years

Had it not been for all the young men being called up, we
would not have gotten the jobs we were able to get.
—Ruth and Ruby Crawford

"During World War II, Atlanta was nothing like it is now. All the boys were
in the service. That's when women started in the work force, because the
men had to go off to war. In Atlanta, some of the women worked in banks and
department stores, and many of them worked as clerks. There were a lot of
ten-cent stores like McCrory's and Woolworth's, and so many of the women
working in those places had been homemakers until they went into the work
force. Some were not well educated and had no business experience, but they
could contribute, and they did."

Ruth and Ruby readily agreed, "You know, that was war time, and if so
many of the men had not been in service, and many overseas, we would likely
have been put in one of those jobs like switchboard operator or stenographer
because that's where a girl started in those days."

The South, and Georgia in particular, was a crucial component in the
American effort to emerge victorious from World War II. More than 320,000
Georgians served in the U.S. military, and hundreds of thousands of people,
men and women, black and white, were employed by the rapidly-expanding war
industries. As the U.S. commitment and eventual all-out involvement in the
war overseas escalated, U.S. war money inundated southern states to build or
improve military installations and war plants. In Georgia, nearly every major
city had a military base or installation of some kind. Columbus hosted Fort
Benning, which quickly became the world's largest infantry training school.
Robins Field near Macon, now Robins Airforce Base, put more than 13,000
civilians to work. More than 2,000 Naval aviators were trained for combat
in Athens at the University of Georgia. Savannah's Hunter Field turned out
Army Air Corps pilots as fast as they could be trained. Fort Gordon, known
in those days as Camp Gordon, brought thousands of soldiers to Augusta for
training before deploying them to duty stations around the world.

Because the weather was generally good and the pool of labor vast, defense
contractors flocked to Georgia with jobs and revenue that saw Georgia's

civilian population explode and contribute greatly to the war effort. The Bell Bomber Plant (or Bell Aviation) at Marietta (now Lockheed Martin) during peak production years employed more than 28,000 Georgians building B-29 Supercruiser high-altitude bombers. There were ordinance plants popping up in Macon, Milledgeville, and other towns across the state. Along the Atlantic coast, "Liberty ships," the troop and supply ships slated to liberate Europe, were turned out at a furious pace. Southeastern Shipbuilding Corporation in Savannah constructed Liberty ships on the Savannah River and provided jobs for thousands of workers. At J. A. Jones Shipyard in Brunswick, ships were constructed six at a time, producing a total of ninety-nine ships in two short years.

Throughout the state, women were beneficiaries of the dramatic increases in employment in commerce and industry. With so many men being shipped out, women entered the workforce in record numbers, many for the first time. Before the war, women comprised less than twenty-four percent of the workforce. By the end, that had grown to close to forty percent. Many women sought and obtained employment in what had been male-dominated industries like munitions factories, foundries, industrial plants, banks, and financial institutions. Wartime employment for women was something of a paradox, occurring in a tightly controlled system that upheld existing gender biases while at the same time giving women responsibilities that had always been reserved for men.

"Now the men weren't all gone, and there were some very good ones at the bank," Ruth recounted. "But the bank was shorthanded of men and we could do the work. And we had a good introduction. Still, we had to get the job done. Maybe even better than a man would have had to."

After the war, many women "retired," resuming domestic routines and responsibilities. The women who stayed in the workforce were often, though not always, shifted into subordinate positions where salaries were often half those paid to the returning men.

Not all women were happy or able to go back in rank or to being strictly homemakers. One who found herself in the workforce after the war was Mary McKinsey who began operating Mary Mac's Tea Room[5] in 1945. The Tea Room, or Mary Mac's, as it is more commonly known, is an Atlanta landmark and has been a favorite place of the Crawford sisters for decades. In the early 1960s, Margaret Lupo, another enterprising woman, bought Mary Mac's and continued the tradition started by Ms. McKinsey. In later years, because Ruth and Ruby enjoyed Mary Mac's so much and were so well known there, they acted as hostesses when their schedule allowed it. It was women like Ruth and Ruby and the Mary McKinseys and Margaret Lupos of the world who continued working after the war, making differences and pushing for change.

"We liked what we were doing," Ruby recalled. "We loved the people we worked with, and we really enjoyed the jobs we were doing. We had done well, and neither of us saw any reason at all to step aside. We felt we could do as well as anyone."

"Everyone was involved in some way with the war," Ruth remembered. "It was just something that affected everyone and we all tried to do our part as much as we could."

"I remember," Ruby recalled, "some of the experiences we had with some of the GIs when they came back. I used to write a breezy Walter Winchell-type column and one returning soldier told me, 'You just don't know what that column did for us when we read it in our foxholes.' We were delighted about that, and we ended up being editors of that for awhile, too."

"We also were editors of the Women Accountants bulletin, and the Women Lawyers bulletin, and did a lot on the Women's Chamber of Commerce bulletin. So we were sometimes down there at midnight working and the cleaning help would come clean and go home and we'd still be there. Many times we would ride down on the elevator with Mr. J.B. Fuqua of the big conglomerate. He was there because he wanted to be, and we were there because we were just working."

"We told everybody," Ruth said, "that we wound the cat and put out the clock at midnight. We held all the offices, secretary, treasurer, executive vice-president, and president in many of those organizations, and we enjoyed every minute of it, not really considering it work, you know."

"On weekends we went to Temple to be with our Mother and Daddy, and we went to church with them out there and did all those things and then came back to Atlanta to start all over again. We had just five days a week in town, and then back home to Temple."

"But we enjoyed ourselves in Atlanta, and all our Atlanta friends. We went to the All-Star concert series and the shows. They had a lot of good movies then. We also had Tommy Dorsey's Orchestra, and the Capitol Theater, and the Rose Band, and the Paramount, and the Fox, with Judy Canova and people like that."

"And the Paradise Room at the Henry Grady Hotel[6] was the greatest place. They'd have a luncheon and a dinner show there every night with people like Andy Griffith and Dick Van Dyke getting their start there. Really, that was the greatest place to be."

"Back in those days," Ruby recalled, "if you had out-of-town guests, you either took them to the Atlanta Biltmore Hotel or Aunt Fanny's Cabin[7] or

Mammy's Shanty[8] in Atlanta. Or the Paradise Room. That was the big thing. It was the greatest. It was just beautiful and it had wonderful food, and auctions, dancing, everything. You went to the Paradise Room to be in paradise. On Saturdays they had a lot of parties. It was in fashion for just years and years, about twenty years as I recall. It was so popular and well thought of that even Rich's had its business meetings there."

On the loss of Rich's Department Store, an Atlanta institution for decades with its huge Christmas tree, Pink Pig kiddie trains, famous Magnolia Room, and its unusual but endearing customer relations policies,[9] the Crawford sisters agreed that, "Mr. Rich loved that store. Everybody just loved it. We were like a lot of people when it closed—very unhappy. We miss it. Mr. Rich did so much for this community. He was involved in everything. He was involved in every good cause, every civic endeavor, and everything else to help the community. The customer was always right in his store, and he contributed to everything. He made that store what it was."

"This will tell you how much we admire Rich's. Many years ago, Ruth and I and our sister Joan and Daddy were all down at Jekyll Island. We had taken a boat out and a storm came up. There were two men, Moses and Preacher, out there with us. Their boss had flown them out there for the day to take care of some things for him. He was going to fly back out and get them at the end of the day but the weather had gotten so bad that flying was out of the question, so they hitched a ride on the boat with us. We headed out across St. Andrew's Sound, which is full of sharks, and I have never wanted to be shark bait. So we were getting a little nervous. After a while the weather got really bad and I said to the men, 'Moses, you and Preacher need to lead us out of this.' A little while later, when we had on life jackets and it looked like we were going over the side, somebody said to grab our two most valuable possessions. I was asked what besides Ruth was I going to grab. And I said, 'I'm not grabbing Ruth. I'm saving my dog and my Rich's charge card.'"

"For about fifteen years we served on the Rich's Business Women's Fashion Board where we modeled for them. We got to know so many nice people there. And we thought so much of all of them, especially Mr. Rich."

Ruby laughed when remembering that "My friend worked there in public relations. He told me that Mr. Rich said, 'The customer is always right' so much that after a while my friend got to believing it himself."

Ruth and Ruby were not the only loyal customers of Rich's Department Store. The store was founded in 1867 and grew rapidly. When in the early part of the Twentieth Century cotton prices plummeted, Rich's took bales of cotton in exchange for goods. During the Great Depression, when the city of Atlanta could not pay its school teachers, the store negotiated their paychecks nonetheless.

Beginning on Thanksgiving, 1948, the first "Great Tree" was raised on the roof of Rich's downtown Atlanta store in what became known as "The Lighting of the Great Tree" that signaled (as it still does, though under the Macy's banner) the beginning of the holiday season in Atlanta and throughout the South. In 1953, the first Pink Pig, Priscilla, was introduced and became so popular that Percival was drafted soon after and the ride had to be moved outside the store to accommodate the crowds of devoted customers when those trains circled the Great Tree.

Although the world was in a state of great turmoil the 1940s began quietly enough in Georgia. Germany was in the grip of the National Socialist Party, the Battle of Britain had been fought, the Lend-Lease policy was in place, and tensions in the Far East and the Pacific boiled over. On December 7, 1941, Japan attacked American military forces at Pearl Harbor and Hickam Field on the Hawaiian Island of Oahu. The following day, America was at war with Japan, and shortly thereafter, Germany and Italy. It was, and would be for some time, the Allies against the Axis.

During and after the war the political, social, economic, and cultural landscape of America underwent profound changes at every level and in every locale. In Georgia, things changed, sometimes very quickly, in other cases not as rapidly as elsewhere.

The first candidate that the Crawford sisters ever supported, Eugene Talmadge, after having been governor in the Thirties, reemerged as a force in Georgia politics, and not without a little controversy. Reelected Governor in 1940, Talmadge ruffled feathers considerably during the "Cocking Affair"[10] at the University of Georgia and was defeated for reelection in 1942, the only time that he ever lost a gubernatorial contest.

Reelected in 1946, Talmadge died that year before being inaugurated, leading to what became known as the "Three Governors" controversy: The General Assembly elected Talmadge's son Herman governor, even though he had not run for the office; Melvin Thompson, the newly-elected lieutenant governor, claimed the office himself; and outgoing governor Ellis Arnall also staked a claim. The Georgia Supreme Court terminated the controversy by ending the administration of Herman Talmadge and ruling that Thompson should serve as acting governor until the next general election in 1948.

Long-time Crawford friend and Atlanta native William B. Hartsfield was Atlanta's mayor from 1937 to 1941, and again from 1942 to 1962, making him the longest-serving mayor in Atlanta history. Atlanta has long called itself "The city too busy to hate." During the civil rights struggles in ensuing years that legacy, begun by Mayor Hartsfield, served the city very well and made its transition from the old ways to the new ones much easier and more peaceful than that of many other cities, Northern, Southern, Eastern, or Western.

Throughout most of World War II, Franklin Roosevelt was President. America was probably more united then than at any other time in her history. On April 12, 1945, in Warm Springs, Georgia,[11] less than one month before the end of the war in Europe, Roosevelt, just beginning his fourth term, died without ever seeing Germany and Japan surrender. Harry S. Truman was sworn in that day and occupied the office until January of 1953.

At home, especially in the South, Jim Crow[12] was dying, and dying hard in many places. The war brought African-Americans off farms and out of shanty towns to defense industries throughout the South and across the rest of the country. The roots of the Civil Rights Movement that had such profound effect on Atlanta and the rest of the country are to be found in the war years. Manpower shortages, combat requirements, and the insatiable thirst of the American war industry for labor dictated changes that saw black and white men and women working in the same factories and shipyards. Black combat units were formed in all three services and though still segregated proved willing and able to fight. Those units performed at very high levels in all theaters of the war.

Atlanta was a focal point for change, peaceful change. According to Drs. Clarissa Myrick-Harris and Norman Harris of OneWorld Archives, "This discussion of the civil rights movement in Atlanta begins with the decade 1940–1949 [when] black leaders decided that they could best accomplish their goal through slow, deliberate steps rather than trying to force rapid change. Most often, this gradual change was achieved through negotiations between the black leadership and those with influence in the city's white political power structure," among them, William B. Hartsfield.

In that era, baseball was big in Atlanta. The baseball games Ruth and Ruby attended on a regular basis were usually held at the Ponce de Leon Ballpark, a place that is now only a memory.

"We used to love going over to Ponce de Leon Park and watching all those great ballplayers," Ruby recalled. "We had the best time."

Then Atlanta was home to one of the most popular and successful minor league baseball teams in the country, the Atlanta Crackers.[13] Founded in 1901, the team played in Atlanta until 1965. During its sixty-four years as Atlanta's team, the Crackers won seventeen league championships, a feat bested by only one other baseball team, and a *major* league team at that, the New York Yankees. Fans, Ruth and Ruby among them, watched Hall of Famers Luke Appling, Eddie Mathews, Tommie Aaron, along with Tim McCarver and Chuck Tanner, all who began their professional baseball careers with the Crackers, as did Skip Carey and Ernie Harwell, well-known announcers even today.

"In that film we did for public television in Atlanta, *Lost Atlanta: The Way We Were*, we talked a lot about the way things were back then. Things have changed so much since those times. It was all very different then than it is now."

Interviewed for the Georgia Public Broadcasting production, *Lost Atlanta: The Way We Were*, Ruth remembered some venerated Atlanta haunts fondly, like Jacob's Pharmacy, once located in the First National Bank Building at the corner of Marietta and Peachtree Streets. "It had a soda fountain and marvelous breakfasts, and the best chicken salad. Oh, we used to go down in the late afternoon after we'd finished work at the bank and have a chicken salad sandwich, before we had dinner! The chicken salad was marvelous, and the breakfasts, with the grits and the gravy and the scrambled eggs and bacon or sausage … and we loved to go there for breakfast. And at the soda fountain, we'd have banana splits—"

"They had wonderful banana splits," Ruby added, rolling her eyes remembering the pleasant indulgence. Later, she recalled that Jacob's Pharmacy was one of the most popular early-morning haunts for nearly everyone in Atlanta. "Everyone just loved it. They flocked there almost every morning."

Temple Building and Supply was a new building when Ruth and Ruby were growing up in Temple. (Author's Collection)

Reminiscent of the house Ruth and Ruby grew up in, this one is in the same neighborhood. The old family home was "taken down" many years ago. (Author's Collection)

Temple United Methodist Church, Ruth and Ruby's hometown church. (Author's Collection)

This water tower, located at the far western end of old Temple Village, announces Temple's status as a city. Temple was a village when Ruth and Ruby were growing up. (Author's Collection)

Ruby (left) and Ruth flanked by the crew at the Varsity on the 75th anniversary of the Varsity, opened in 1928 by Frank Gordy. (Crawford Collection)

Ruth and Ruby circa 1948, celebrating their admission to the State Bar of Georgia in which they remained active members throughout their lives. (Crawford Collection)

DOUBLE ENTRY FOR BANKERS—The Crawford sisters from Atlanta keep dele-
gates at the American Institute of Banking convention guessing which is which as
they sip their morning coffee. Identical twins who dress alike, both are lawyers and
both are concerned with the trust phase of banking. Ruby, left, is manager of the
corporate trust department and Ruth, right, is trust auditor of the First National
Bank, Atlanta. —Times Herald Staff Photo.

At the American Institute of Banking in Chicago. (Crawford Collection)

Glamorous Ruth.
(Crawford Collection)

Scads of azaleas in the back yard at the sisters' Narmore Street home in Buckhead. Ruth and Ruby, inveterate and intrepid gardeners since childhood, planted, cultivated, and fussed over every living thing in that yard, and the yards in their other places on Jekyll Island, Lake Rabun, and the lake house near Temple. (Crawford Collection)

Ruth (seated) with Ruby at her back in Senator Herman Talmadge's Washington, D.C. office. (Crawford Collection)

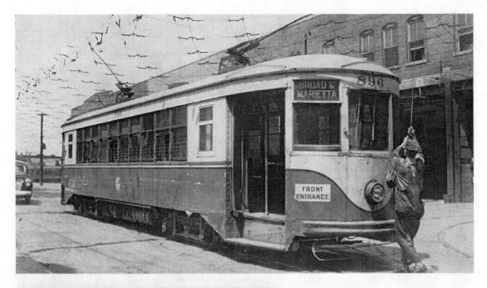

Number 896 Street Car bound for the intersection of Broad and Marietta Streets in Atlanta circa 1945. Ruth and Ruby rode the street cars, as did many Atlantans, everywhere until the trolleys were finally retired in the mid-1960s. (Courtesy of Bill Volkmer from the Bill Volkmer Collection with kind permission)

Easter! (Crawford Collection)

Ruby (left) and Ruth acting as hostesses in the revived Mary Mac's Tea Room on Ponce de Leon Avenue in downtown Atlanta. This same photo resides somewhere among the many photos of Ruth and Ruby that adorn the walls at Mary Mac's Tea Room in Atlanta. (Crawford Collection and Mary Mac's Collection with kind permission)

Ruby (left) and Ruth (right) preparing to make soup for the homeless and needy. "First you start with 150 pounds of top sirloin ...." (Crawford Collection)

In October 1954, when Ruth and Ruby were in New York for national meeting of accountants and CPAs, they were asked to appear on the popular celebrity game show, *What's My Line?* They stumped the panel as the twin women lawyers. (Crawford Collection)

Ruth and Ruby at the national convention of the Association of Women Accountants, circa 1965. (Crawford Collection)

DEAR Ruth & Ruby *(Please excuse me my pen! I am out of stationery & pens!)*

I WANTED TO WRITE AND TELL you HOW much I APPRECIATE YOUR GIFT OF A BRAVES PENNANT T-SHIRT. Your GIFT WAS ANOTHER INDICATION OF your MARVELOUS GENEROSITY AND KINDNESS. And ESPECIALLY TOWARD your PREACHERS! you HAVE BEEN SO GOOD TO ME & my FAMILY. CAROL, AMANDA, & I ARE GRATEFUL TO YOU BOTH.

And this note also gives ME an OPPORTUNITY TO EXPRESS TO you my GRATITUDE FOR your PRESENCE in our FAMILY OF FAITH here at Jekyll. You make such an impact, as you do at Peachtree Road and at Temple. One of the authentic joys of this ministry is the opportunity to meet, come to know, and work with persons like you who love the LORD and His Church.

IT IS A PRIVILEGE AND AND HONOR TO CALL you FRIENDS AND SISTERS IN CHRIST. your REMARKABLE LIVES, your MANY GROUND-BREAKING ACHIEVEMENTS ARE WELL-KNOWN. Your LIVES OF SERVICE TO OTHERS, your STRUGGLES FOR JUSTICE, your ENDURING WITNESS, HAVE BEEN MARKED BY A GRACIOUS SPIRIT, A LOVING SENSITIVITY, AND A COURAGE THAT ALWAYS INSPIRES ALL WHO KNOW you. Your COMBINATION OF GAIETY AND DIGNITY is UNFORTUNATELY A FAST-FADING ATTRIBUTE, A LOST ART IN AN AGE TOO BUSY, TOO UNDISCIPLINED, TOO SELFISH TO CARE. PERHAPS, THOUGH, THE ATTRIBUTE/QUALITY PERSONS MOST ADMIRE IS your DESIRE TO ENCOURAGE OTHERS. MORE THAN MOST ANYONE I KNOW, you TWO EXEMPLIFY THE BALANCED LIFE OF FAITH & WORKS, RIGHTEOUSNESS & JUSTICE, WORSHIP AND ACTION, CHRIST TAUGHT.

Too, you ARE FUN! FOR OTHERS, IN A WORLD IN WHICH MOST OF US TAKE OURSELVES FAR TOO SERIOUSLY, Laughter is a gift, a healing gift. You give that gift in great measure ~

WELL, ENOUGH OF THAT. I'm SURE you HEAR THAT OFTEN. I JUST WANTED you TO KNOW HOW much you HAVE ENRICHED my LIFE ~ AS you HAVE SO MANY COUNTLESS OTHERS.

Thanks again ~ many thanks ~ You are in my prayers, THESE DAYS ESPECIALLY. May God richly bless you in every way, now & always. THE BRAVES ~ in this early Friday morn HAVE JUST won GAME 5. CAN THE MAGIC continue? "You Gotta Believe!" BESIDES, you survived OPRAH! I know now what you MEANT ABOUT THE SNOW!

I hope to SEE you SOON ~

GRACE & PEACE,
Tom

A handwritten letter of thanks to Ruth and Ruby for their hard work and stewardship from a dear friend and minister with whom they worked. The sisters were particularly proud of these kinds of letter of which they received many over their lifetimes. (Crawford Collection)

Ruby stirring a ten-gallon pot of soup. (Crawford Collection)

Ruby (left) and Ruth at a meeting of the American Bar Association of which they were the only twin women members for many years. (Crawford Collection)

Ruth with Christmas presents around 1952.
(Crawford Collection)

Ruby (holding Celebrity) and Ruth circa 1965. (Crawford Collection)

Ruby and Ruth (holding Celebrity) for a "family" portrait. (Crawford Collection)

Ruth and Ruby and Kandy and Kisses with Santa. They were always good little girls and boys. (Crawford Collection)

Celebrity, Ruth, and Ruby at home. (Crawford Collection)

Ruby and Ruth with twin beagles from a Atlanta Humane Society "Adopt-a-Pet" day.
(Crawford Collection)

Ruth and Ruby flanking Arthur and Stephanie Blank at the 1996 "No Ball at All" held by the Atlanta Humane Society where $60,000 was raised. (Crawford Collection)

For Ruth and Ruby hospitality was a given. Here Ruby receives the Hospitality Award.. (Crawford Collection)

Colorful and stylish twin sisters circa 1960. (Crawford Collection)

Ruth and Ruby at Mary Mac's Tea Room. (Crawford Collection)

Ruth and Ruby and The Gracious Ladies of Georgia. Being Gracious Ladies of Georgia was a distinction they wore with great pride and humility. (Crawford Collection)

Ruth (left) and Ruby sporting recently-won medals for Kandi and Kisses in a competition the name of which escaped Ruby. (Crawford Collection)

Christmas with Kandi and Kisses and Ruby. (Crawford Collection)

Santa's Helpers. (Crawford Collection)

Ruby (left) and Ruth flank Roselle Fabiani, founder of The Gracious Ladies of Georgia. (Crawford Collection)

Ruby (left) and Ruth at The Gracious Ladies of Georgia Christmas celebration. (Crawford Collection)

PEANUT BRIGADE — Five Georgians working in Keene this week for President Jimmy Carter's re-election campaign are, from left, M.C. Wicht, Ruby Crawford, Louis Lefkoff, Nina Jackson and Bobby Kahn. (Sentinel Photo — Manlove)

Georgia Volunteers Taking
To Keene Streets for Carter

By GEORGE MANLOVE
Sentinel Staff Writer

They left the warmth of Georgia last Saturday, and have caught the brunt of the chilliest week so far this season in Keene, but they insist they don't mind the cold.

The "Peanut Brigade" from Georgia is now pounding the streets in Keene in support of President Jimmy Carter's re-election bid.

Five of the 78 Georgians who are canvassing New Hampshire for the Carter-Mondale campaign are spending this week in Keene.

They've been visiting houses of registered Democrats throughout the city, passing out holiday wishes and taking what they say is a soft-sell campaign approach.

They're also trying to gauge how popular the incumbent president from Georgia seems to be.

Some Peanute Bridagers were in New Hampshire in 1976, also campaigning for Carter. Some are retired, all seem enthusiastic, and they have bundled up warmly against cold weather they're not used to.

On Monday, the group seemed euphoric over the response to the Carter campaign which they have seen so far. The Georgians say Carter has a 2-1 lead over U.S. Sen. Edward M. Kennedy among Keene Democrats.

"Practically no one thumbs their nose at us and says, 'Kennedy,'" said Louis Lefkoff of Atlanta.

Sometime this week, many Keene Democrats can expect to find a smiling Georgian at their door, dressed in the Carter colors of green and white, offering season's greetings with a southern drawl.

"We love it in New Hamp-

shire," said Ruby Crawford, a lawyer from Atlanta. "The streets are cold, but the hearts are warm."

The Georgians are staying with several Keene families and will work 14-hour days through Saturday, rallying support for Carter.

Their temporary headquarters are in the Carter Re-Election Campaign office at 23 West St. When the Georgians leave Keene Sunday, though, pro-Carter campaigning won't stop.

Patricia T. Russell of 74 Beech St., a state legislator from Ward 2, has been coordinating the Keene-area campaign, and said Monday that the Peanut Brigade marked the beginning of door-to-door campaigning in Keene by Carter volunteers.

She expects other Carter representatives next month, probably Carter's son Chip and maybe Carter's mother, Miss Lillian Carter.

A clipping from *The Keene* [New Hampshire] *Sentinel* introducing Ruby and other members of the Peanut Brigade during the 1976 campaign for Jimmy Carter's presidency.

Ruth's (seated) office at the First National Bank of Atlanta circa 1955. (Crawford Collection)

Ruby (left) listens while Ruth tells Governor Sonny Perdue what is on their minds. (Crawford Collection)

One of many celebrations with President Jimmy Carter. (Crawford Collection with the kind permission of the Carter Center)

Ruth and their dear friend former Georgia Governor Lester Maddox. (Crawford Collection)

Ruth and Ruby campaigned heavily for Jimmy Carter in 1976 as members of his "Peanut Brigade." Twin poodles Kandi and Kisses traveled with them whenever possible.

The sisters have always loved hats. "We wish they'd come back in style again," they say.

virtues of staying busy. "Our mother could think up more things for us to do than anybody you ever saw," they recall. "People don't know how we can live and do all the things we do, but that is just how we were raised."

Another secret of their success—the twins are avowed night owls ("the higher the moon, the wider our eyes," they claim) who go to bed between 1:30 and 4 a.m. and rise at 8 a.m. Despite their short hours of slumber, they work all day and socialize all night with ease.

"They can stay up half the night and still get up and go," declares John Ferrell, owner of Mary Mac's Tea room in Atlanta and a close friend. "Whenever I see them at parties, they always have two other events to attend—at least."

But their active social life is more than mere pleasure: They are key workers for several charities and are highly sought guests at fundraisers. Ruth and Ruby are especially active members of their church, Peachtree Road United Methodist. "One of our stewards asked if we had a bed at the church," Ruth says. "I said, 'no, but we need one!' "

They feed the hungry as part of the church's outreach committee (Ruby has cooked for up to 650 people at one time) and call on people who are sick or in trouble. At fundraising events, they serve as cashiers.

Then there are Humane Society fundraisers, the Atlanta Union Mission, United Way activities, volunteer work at the Peachtree Center and the Carter Center (both women are lifelong Democrats), and visits with the bereaved. Having so many friends requires frequent trips to the funeral home, Ruby says. "When I die, they won't have to take me to Springhill Mortuary," she laughs, "I'll already be there."

Such unfailing kindness and commitment are Ruth and Ruby Crawford's hallmarks. "Every morning, our prayer for the day is to be of service to as many people as we can—to be kind, thoughtful, compassionate, and considerate," they say. Our mother and father taught us to be honest and to be people of integrity, and when we are, we honor them."

"We just want to make a difference," Ruby adds. When we're gone, I just hope someone remembers."   —Donna Florio

Atlanta Magazine clipping of Ruth and Ruby and Kandi and Kisses with President Carter, and the red Cadillac (one of a red and blue pair) along with other clipping from the Crawford Collection. (With kind permission)

Ruth and Ruby visit the White House after the January 20, 1977 Inauguration of James Earl Carter as our 39th President. (Crawford Collection)

Ruby and Ruth and Rosalyn and President Jimmy Carter are in this signed photo in which the caption reads, "Best Wishes to Ruth and Ruby Crawford Jimmy Carter & Rosalyn Carter." (Crawford Collection and with the kind permission of the Carter Center.)

Ruth and Ruby at a Charity Yard Sale put on by Northside Realty to raise money for needy and homeless people. (Crawford Collection)

Easter at Peachtree Road United Methodist Church. (Crawford Collection)

Ruth and Ruby with 1985 Miss Georgia Stephanie Mohr at the Gracious Ladies of Georgia Annual Cotillion. (Crawford Collection)

This clipping commemorates the founding of the School of Esoteric Art, one of many Crawford civic causes. (Crawford Collection)

Ruth (left) and Ruby at their duties as realtors for Northside Realty. (Crawford Collection)

DOUBLE ACHIEVEMENT

The 2004 Siegel Institute for Leadership, Ethics & Character Phenomenal Woman of the Year Award was conferred upon Ruth and Ruby by Dr. Betty Siegel, President Emeritus of Kennesaw State University. (Crawford Collection)

Photo special to The Marietta Daily Journal

A highlight of the day at the fourth annual Phenomenal Women's Conference presented by RTM Institute for Leadership, Ethics and Character at Kennesaw State University, was the presentation of the Jeanne B. Cook Phenomenal Woman's Award to Atlanta twins Ruth and Ruby Crawford. Both Ruth and Ruby gave entertaining acceptance speeches that outlined how women's roles have changed over the years, with examples from their own noteworthy and varied careers. Above: Ruth Crawford, Kennesaw State University president Dr. Betty Siegel and Ruby Crawford are shown.

Ruth and Ruby (far right, standing) with the STAR students at Jekyll Island. (Crawford Collection)

Ringing in the sheaves. Ruth and Ruby passing the collection plate at Peachtree Road United Methodist Church in Atlanta. (Crawford Collection)

Peachtree Road United Methodist Church where Ruth and Ruby regularly stationed themselves for over three decades to watch the annual 4th of July AJC Peachtree Road Race. (Author's Collection)

No "retirement" for Ruby and Ruth Crawford. Both ladies looked after their civic and church activities until failing health prevented them from continuing. Ruby said on the occasion of the death of her sister, "I guess I'll have to pull double duty now." By all accounts she did so. (Crawford Collection)

The famous "Van" and the patio at their lake house near Temple, Georgia. (Crawford Collection)

Ruth and Ruby enjoying their "retirement." (Crawford Collection)

All dressed up in pink—a favorite Crawford Sisters color—Ruth and Ruby celebrate their 82nd birthday. (Crawford Collection)

The Crawford house on Jekyll Island. (Crawford Collection)

The beach at Jekyll Island where the Crawford sisters spent many enjoyable hours. (Crawford Collection)

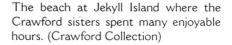

The Crawford house on Jekyll Island from the yard. (Crawford Collection)

Hundreds stop to greet, hug, kiss, shake hands, and have their pictures taken with Ruth and Ruby here in 2005. (Author's Collection)

Start of the 2005 annual AJC Peachtree Road Race. Ruth and Ruby attended the race together, all but one year when Ruby was ill, from the second race in 1971 until 2005. (Author's Collection)

In the finest and most colorful patriotic garb, Ruth and Ruby, at the 2005 AJC Peachtree Road Race cheer on the runners of all ability levels as they had for thirty-three years. (Author's Collection)

More of the same. The greeting of the twins by race participants started very early in the race and continued while the fifty-or-so thousands passed by. (Author's Collection)

This last photograph taken of Ruth and Ruby together at the AJC Peachtree Road Race. (Author's Collection)

Ruth Marion Crawford 1919–2005

Ruby Marie Crawford 1919–2009

Chapter Six

Sticking With It Through the 1950s

We just kept studying and trying to make ourselves the best qualified.

—Ruth and Ruby Crawford

Many of the gains women made in businesses or industries traditionally dominated by men began to be lost after the war and into the 1950s. Returning servicemen created competition and some women simply went home. Others who were engaged in their work and determined to continue making contributions stayed on. It was not easy for those women. Advancement, when it did come, came slowly. And there was an innate predisposition to think that somehow women who did the same work as men were not deserving of the same pay.

Recalling promotions and opportunities in the bank, the sisters agreed, "They were few and far between for women."

Ruth and Ruby managed to do what they did because, as Ruby tells it, "We just kept on studying and trying to make ourselves the best qualified. If anything new came along, like computers have nowadays, we tried to learn about it and be up-to-date on everything—"

"Back then everything was IBM," Ruth remembered, "and we learned it; even though we really didn't have to learn how to use the systems, we did. And we just kept doing what we were doing as well as we could do it."

"It took a lot of faith that right would prevail," Ruby says. "And we had faith that eventually promotions would come, that things would change for women."

"Did they ever?" Ruth wonders. "Some. But, completely, where women have exactly the same opportunities as men, no. They still haven't."

"Even though our little ol' daddy used to tell us we should find something else, we stayed with the bank."

"The truth is, we just loved it. It was a challenge. We just wanted to make a difference. Many times Daddy tried to get us to leave. He'd say, 'You need to get out and make money for yourselves. Don't work for the other fellow.'"

"He had always been in business for himself and he always said, 'Make the money for yourself.' But it just became a challenge. We were determined to make a difference for women in the banking business."

"And you know what? We did. They really do thank us now," Ruth said.

"We've been to all kinds of meetings and other gatherings over the years in the banking organizations we belong to, and women come up to us, some of whom weren't even born when we were getting started, and they are so sweet to express their appreciation to us."

"At the time discrimination was difficult to take. But we really loved banking so much, and we loved the people we worked with. We just had the greatest people. We thought about leaving several times when we were offered other jobs, but we never left."

"We were offered jobs by other banks. Even the bank in Temple talked to me about making me the president," Ruth remembered. "And I was very interested, and complimented, too. Because, even though it was a small town bank, it would have been, and I want to say this properly, in effect, my bank. But in the end I decided that I'd rather be an officer at First National Bank of Atlanta, the largest in the Southeast, than president of a smaller institution. And, we had given so much to the bank already that we felt like we ought to stick it out."

During those years Ruby began teaching classes in banking and law. The American Bankers Association, through its educational arm the American Institute of Banking or AIB,[14] has for many years conducted classes for executives and officers of America's banking institutions.

Ruby, reflecting upon her years as a teacher, reminisced, "I taught bankers for sixteen years and also lectured in estate planning out at Emory Law School as a guest lecturer. I also taught some of the evening courses at Emory that Mary Cobb Bugg Callahan started, all those 'Evening at Emory' education courses that they have out there now. I taught Law for the Layman and Law for Business and Professional Women. I must have done that for about eight years or more at the YWCA and also at the Kennedy-Sinclair Trust Institute in New York."

"I've always said that I had the best students in the world. For some of the courses, many were bankers. In New York, bankers from all over the United States studied employee-benefit plans and HR 10s and CO plans and all that. That's what I lectured on at Kennedy-Sinclair. I was in on the embryonic stages at the bank in setting up retirement plans. Estate planning was always my specialty. That was an area where I represented the bank."

Ruth, recalling Ruby's years as a teacher, noted that, "She taught banking to people who were just like we were when we started out, young bankers. Many of the future CEOs were in her classes, too. The CEOs could be graduates of Harvard or some other Ivy League School, but they had to take Principles of Banking, Commercial Law, and those types of courses. They weren't easy, I can tell you that. Even though many of the new bankers had fine educations, they all had to take the AIB courses if they wanted to get the proper certificates. It didn't matter where they had gone to school."

"Richard Katrel," Ruby recalled, "was a delightful person and an excellent banker who didn't live long. He died at an early age. When they made him president of his bank, I said, 'Oh Richard, see what they made you? See what they made you after you took my course?' He took Commercial Law and Negotiable Instruments from me. I said, 'They didn't make you president before you took my courses, now did they?' He laughed. He thought that was very funny."

"And when I taught those courses, it didn't make any difference whether the student was a man or a woman," she continued. "Teaching those courses, that's how I got to know so many CEOs, presidents, and senior vice-presidents. I had the most successful classes. They didn't want you to have but about twenty people in a class, but I had as many as sixty in mine, which meant a lot more papers to grade. And the classes weren't easy, either. There was a high attrition rate in the classes throughout the U. S. and I was selected to try to solve that problem because I was one of the most successful teachers and rarely had anyone drop out. So Dean Henry Engler of Loyola University and I went on a speaking engagement to other cities where the AIB held classes, telling the AIB instructors how we conducted our classes and what it took to be a successful teacher and have a big class finish all the course work. That was a big order for me. We went all over the country speaking about how we did it."

"Ruby was teaching the same people who were discriminating against us. They were the CEOs, presidents, and so on who set the policies in the industry. The powers that be."

"It is ironic when you think about it. That we would be teaching banking to people who set the policies that we were struggling to overcome."

"Was there outright discrimination?" they ask each other. "Yes, it was outright," Ruth related. "A woman might be more qualified and have a better education, but men got the jobs and promotions, and the increases in salary. A man with a BA degree from Georgia State would be paid more than they paid me, a woman with three degrees. They would say that a man with a family needs more pay. It didn't matter if there were single mothers with children; men still got more."

"That was not exclusive to the First National Bank of Atlanta," Ruth continued. "All of business was that way then. We stayed with the bank for thirty-three years. In thirty-three years Ruby went from bookkeeping to the Trust Department to Senior Trust Officer and I went from bookkeeping to the Savings Department and the to the Auditing Department as a Trust Auditor. So advancement was possible, just very slow."

Ruth reflected humorously, "As an Auditing Officer, my job was to keep an eye on what they did in the Trust Department, Ruby's department. I used to laugh and tell them that I was there to make sure they all stayed out of jail. I managed to do that," she joked.

"People would come to me sometimes and complain about Ruth. They'd say to me, 'Your sister gives me a such hard time,' and I'd tell them, 'You only have to deal with her eight hours a day. I live with her.' Ruth would always laugh and tell them, 'You need listen to me, now; I'm the one making sure you do things right.'"

Ruby went on to explain that some of the prejudices at the bank were of a more subtle, behind-the-scenes nature. "When I was being promoted, the head of the department said to me, 'You won't have any special favors.' I said, 'I've never asked for any.' And he said, 'Everything will be like it has been.' And then I asked about 'equal pay.' With his eyes spitting fire and his face turning crimson he said, 'Young lady, you will go a lot further in this bank if you never bring that up again.' I never received the equal pay nor was I given the title of Vice-President the male officer I was replacing had held. I got all his work, in addition to my own, but that was it. We didn't have the EEOC in those days. I couldn't do anything about it except leave, and that was something I didn't want to do."

"Since that time, and that was just the way things were in those days," Ruth added, "banks have women in more positions overall now, and in higher-level positions, and they pay much better than they used to. The salaries are higher now for women, but they're still not equal."

"The prejudice that was most hurtful, I think, was lack of equal pay. It would have been easier to take, oh yes, if they paid us the same as they paid men for the same or less demanding work. That was really insulting," Ruby continued. "Now, I know that money can't buy happiness. But, it can buy your way into some of the better places where you can enjoy your misery more."

"Ruth and I were also charter members of the Atlanta Chapter of the American Society of Women Accountants, founded in 1944. We each served in various offices and as president of the organization. The Atlanta Chapter won the National Trophy, a beautiful big silver punch bowl, as the Most

Outstanding chapter in the U. S. during each of our terms as President. Ruth also served on the National Board as Chapter Development Chairman and I spoke at several of our national conventions on tax-related matters."

"I represented the bank," Ruby recalled, "wherever it should be seen. I spoke at the Alabama Bankers Association, National Association of Women Accountants and CPAs. I spoke at the AIB, and The American Bankers Association in New York decided that they wanted us to do some PR work for them. I enjoyed those speaking engagements, and I always had a couple of rules I followed whenever we took one. One was that a good speech has a good beginning and a good end, and both of them are close together. I also believe that when you're asked to speak you should stand up to be seen, speak up to be heard, and sit down to be appreciated."

"They selected us to go around the country and speak on banking as a career," Ruth remembered. "So we did a lot of radio and TV shows and call-in shows and talk shows in New York, Washington, New Orleans, San Diego, and even Mexico, trying to talk people into banking as a career. They chose us and we enjoyed doing it. That was quite an honor. Out of all the banking women in the U. S., they chose the two of us. We were quite pleased that we got to do that. They thought that we were super-bankers and that banking was a super profession. I guess we talked about that so much that we got to believing it ourselves," she laughed. "Maybe we got a little brainwashed into believing it was a great career."

"We did have some misgivings about it, yes, but we loved banking so much, and I had faith that it would not always be that way–discriminatory. But for men it certainly was a good occupation."

"We had a friend in Atlanta whose niece heard our program in New York and told her mother, 'Oh, Mother, I want to start working in a bank.' And she did."

"She didn't take my course because she was in New York. But she heard our program in New York, and she knew we were friends of her uncle in Atlanta. And I guess that did it."

As the 1950s opened, Atlanta was vibrant and growing. Mayor William B. Hartsfield would hold the mayor's office throughout the decade and into the next. Mayor Hartsfield was instrumental in turning Atlanta's airport into an important domestic and international resource and one of the busiest in the country. Hartsfield's 1925 acquisition, Candler Field, had been renamed Atlanta Municipal Airport in 1946. By 1948, the war surplus hangar that Atlanta Municipal used as a terminal saw more than a million people pass through it.[15] So pervasive has the Mayor's creation become, that it is said in the South that even those heading for Heaven (or elsewhere) have to pass through Atlanta on the way. The development of Atlanta as a center for civil aviation, and its successive improvements, has been an important element in opening the national stage for Atlanta, the South, and for Ruth and Ruby Crawford. It would, in the coming years, make it very easy for Atlantans to get to any city in the country, and they, including Ruth and Ruby Crawford did just that.

In the mid to late 1950s, the Governor's mansion was occupied by Samuel Marvin Griffin, viewed by many as the heir apparent to Herman Talmadge who served two terms between 1947 and 1955. On the national and international stage, the War in Korea wound down, and Dwight D. Eisenhower, "Ike," became President in 1953. That year the world was able to see through the new medium of television the coronation of twenty-five-year-old Princess Elizabeth of England as Queen Elizabeth II.

Televison, the new force asserting itself in America, found Atlanta on the cutting edge, just as it had been for television's predecessor, radio. On September 29, 1948, WSB-TV became the first Atlanta station to sign on the air.

"Well, I suppose we had the first TV set in Temple, Georgia," Ruth reminisces in *Lost Atlanta: The Way We Were*. "We gave our mother and daddy a set as soon as they became available on the market, and I remember that we would have neighbors who would come to our house. We'd fill the whole house up with people who came to watch TV."

"We'd set it up theater-style," Ruby says "you know, because everybody in town was so thrilled we were having television, they'd come down to the house and watch it. So, it was great fun having them. Of course, they eventually got television sets of their own, but it was fun. We just enjoyed all the programs and there was just a wonderful [assortment of shows] ... back then. To think that you had television and all the variety shows and the entertainment. It was great."

"I can't remember," Ruby later recalled, "whether we had a Philco first or an RCA. Ford Motor Company made the Philco, you know, the one with the round screen. I know we had an RCA somewhere along the line. I seem to remember the first one had that round screen. So, it may have been a Philco."

As great as it was to see all those events through the eye of television, the stability enjoyed in America in the 1950s, that still causes so many to wax nostalgic for the time, was coming to an end. Beneath the surface, much like under the plates of the Earth's surface, tension, friction, and heat were building in America, in Georgia, and in Atlanta. Those forces would reach a critical and often explosive state in the next decade.

Chapter Seven

Vegetable Beef Soup

First, start with a hundred and fifty pounds of top sirloin
beef tips …

—Ruby Crawford

In addition to their professional and business achievements and many civic
interests, church involvement for the Crawford sisters, whether in Atlanta,
Temple, or wherever they might happen to be, has always been a part of the
mix. Each lady has held nearly every lay position any church had to offer or
would ask one to take. Both Ruth and Ruby have served on more task forces,
committees, groups, commissions, and organizations dedicated to stewardship
and community service than either could easily remember.

"At the church," Ruth recollected, "we're greeters, ushers, and served on the
Administrative Board. We're stewards, it's as simple as that. We'd do all the
cashiering for the social events in the church, we'd meet with the ministers,
we counted money on first Sundays and ushered on third Sundays of the
month. We worked on the Music and Arts Committee and the Flower Guild,
the Outreach Committee, and cashiered the Yard Sale. We've done just about
everything except preach and play the organ."

"Our church in Atlanta is Peachtree Road United Methodist Church," Ruby added.

"But if it's Sunday," Ruth said, "we're in church, no matter where we might
be. Even when we were in Hawaii and Los Angeles, the first thing we did was
go to church, even before we got into our hotel."

Ruby recalled, "Community volunteer work, that is our love; helping
people every way that we can, as long as we can, and everywhere that we can,
especially the homeless and hungry people. Like our daddy, we can't stand to
see somebody hungry. Our church twice a year goes down to Trinity Church
and feeds the street people down there, and we helped with that. We also have
the Buckhead Christian Ministry where we hand out food and clothes and
also try to set them up in apartments and get them back on their feet with
jobs. We have two drives a year at our church where we collect and distribute
groceries to people for a month. It started out with four or five churches, but
now we have maybe twenty or so involved. It got so big that they have a new
home now over on Piedmont Avenue."

"Ruby and I are interested in helping everybody that we can and to be of service to as many people as we can. Mother and Daddy taught us to be givers and not takers. I feel like what you have in life is what you give, and I have always felt like community service and giving back is part of the rent you pay for being here."

A common lament among those who dedicate themselves to civic causes are those members who align themselves with organizations, building a résumé of civic affiliations, yet doing little more than paying dues and attending an occasional meeting or a very public function or two. That complaint could never be leveled at the Crawford sisters. Ruth and Ruby have been members of the Atlanta Humane Society for more than thirty years, and Ruby did a great deal of volunteer legal work for the Humane Society for many of those years and served on the Board of Directors for over thirty-five years. Additionally, they served as docents at the Carter Center, doing, as Ruth said, "Whatever needs to be done out there."

As members of the Buckhead Christian Ministry and the Feed the Hungry Project, Ruth and Ruby have been co-chairs of that organization and have helped raise another $125,000 to feed the hungry. The sisters were also honorary co-chairmen and helped raise $125,000 for North Fulton Senior Citizen Services.

Ruth explained, "That's a place that provides companionship, entertainment, and activities for elderly citizens of North Fulton County and the surrounding area."

Well into their own "retirement" by some three decades, the sisters report, "That's where seniors go during the day and can do all these things. They are picked up by bus and taken there where they can take part in all kinds of activities, discussions, keep up with current events, with their friends. The good thing is that they are able to keep moving, making new friends, and keeping company with people of their own generation. It really is a great service."

"We go visit a lot of people like that. It does them so much good, and it's good for us, too."

"We feel so strongly about it that we've often said," Ruth joked, "that if you're below the age of eighty, you might not have much of a chance of seeing us at all."

"We're not joiners," Ruth often said. "If we can't do something, we're not going to be part of whatever it is. We believe it's important to contribute."

Ruby proudly tells of the two of them making ten ten-gallon pots of soup at a time for a total of a hundred gallons—enough to feed 700 people. Ruby and Ruth stirred the pots themselves with implements the size of canoe paddles. Ruby related the story of a young man who was particularly taken with her soup. "He wanted to meet the lady who made that soup, you know, meet the chef. I said, 'Bring him back to the kitchen.' So they brought him back. I was stirring soup. We had those big paddle-like things stirring down in that big ten-gallon pot. I shook hands with him and he said, 'Oh, Miss Crawford, I am in the food line every day of my life and your soup is the best soup I have ever eaten in all my life. I don't have a place to live and I don't have a job, but I'm going to get a job and get a place to live, and then I want to have my friends in and I want to make them some soup just exactly like you make your soup. Would you give me your recipe?' I told him of course I would, and I felt really touched by that."

"What is that recipe?" Ruth asked her.

"The recipe? Well, first you start with a hundred and fifty pounds of top sirloin beef tips. Then you add all kinds of vegetables, beans, and carrots, and onions, and peppers get added to that meat. It's so thick it's more like a stew than soup, but very nourishing."

"The people at church like to say that," Ruth reported with a laugh, "'you don't eat Ruby's soup with a spoon, you eat it with a knife and fork.'"

"There are people who say you should feed hungry people with a bologna sandwich, but I don't call that nourishing," Ruby added emphatically. "I want them to have something that is nourishing so they feel full. So they have all that, soup and sandwiches and dessert–pies and things like that. We'd get the soup started and make it so thick it will hardly stir. I joke around and say that after that you just add water until you get a hundred gallons."

"We have to stand on tiptoe just to stir those big pots of soup," Ruth adds, "and we're not tall, so we have to reach up to keep stirring. And the more things Ruby adds, the thicker it gets, and the harder it gets to stir. Sometimes she adds extra potatoes, or macaroni, something to get it to stick to their ribs."

"Well," Ruby recalled, "don't you know that a little later on we were cleaning up one day after feeding a big bunch of people and that young man I gave the recipe to come back to see me. He told me that he had found a job, had a new place to live, and had a place for his friends to come in for soup. I told him how happy that made me, and how much I thought of him coming back to see me. We were finished up by then, and one of the ladies helping asked me when we were going to finally give up all that hard work making that soup."

"I told her 'I'll quit making soup when I stop hearing stories like that.'"

"We get back over to Temple quite often. We were there for homecoming just a few weeks ago. At the church. We still have property out there, so we go just about every week. Just like we've been doing all these years."

"We drive everywhere we go, but we don't have the two Cadillacs anymore."

A number of years before, when the sisters were very heavily engaged in entertaining, hosting parties, receptions, dinner parties, and so on, and, truth told, doing very well professionally, each had a Cadillac. One was blue and the other white, and with their dogs, Kandi and Kisses, "We would just go visit people."

"Oh, I should say we did and we still do. We like to say that we make more hospital calls than any doctor in town. We keep up with the sick. We are interested in them and we send them cards and take them flowers and fruit and food, visit with them and call and check on them. We think that everybody should do something for somebody every day that they live."

Ruth said of her morning spiritual exercise: "I make a prayer every morning after I thank God for another day of life. My prayer is always, 'Lord, make me a blessing today.' Ruby does the same thing. We've been doing that since we were children."

"Some people never do anything for anybody," Ruby observes, "and I think in the end they hurt themselves. It just makes you feel so good and you are just a happier person if you stay busy and do something for someone and think of others and not just yourself. Just make a telephone call. Some people are so wounded; they just appreciate a call."

"Or take them to lunch," Ruth adds, "or for a walk in the park, or sit and read to them or talk to them, or go to the nursing home and visit, and take them a flower. It doesn't have to be a dozen roses. Just anything. Just do something for somebody every day. There are so many lonely people in nursing homes and they sit there all day bored to death because they don't have anybody to talk to or anything to do and nobody comes to see them. It's just depressing."

"People enjoy home-cooked meals. I know when Betty Talmadge had that leg amputated out at Emory, we went out to see her and we asked her, 'What can we do for you, Betty? What would you like to have?' She said, 'I'd like to have some good homemade soup.' So we went home and cooked it and took it out there to her. It's just things like that people appreciate."

"Another friend of ours was dying at hospice. She had cancer, and they just don't want anything to eat. We would take her food. So I asked her, 'Patty, what can I fix for you? What do you think of that you might like to eat?' She said, 'Some rutabaga turnips.' So we went home and fixed them. She was only able to eat just a few bites, but they made her so happy and let her feel just a little bit better for a little while. All she had to do to get them was to just say she wanted them."

"Everybody has just twenty-four hours a day, but you do with your time pretty much what you want to do with it. You find a way. If you really want to do it you can find the time."

"We always like to say," Ruth states, "that the trouble with doing nothing is you never know when you're finished."

In the 1950s, political and social change was occurring from one end of America to the other, and Atlanta was very much a part of it. The Fifties were the bumper crop years of what became known as "the Baby Boom," an era of growth in the economy and the population that officially stretched from 1946 to 1964. America was on an upswing economically. Suburbs and subdivisions were symbols of recovery and a return to stability and normalcy. In that climate, banking was integral and growing rapidly, to the distinct benefit of the institutions and to people like Ruth and Ruby.

In the background of the very busy lives of the Crawford sisters, America, Georgia, and Atlanta were changing again. Entertainment was becoming an industry unto itself with the introduction of television and the skyrocketing recording industry. New types of music and artists appealed directly to America's young people. Movie makers began to target teenage audiences and, depending upon who is doing the telling, to either reflect or direct their social outlook and point of view. A collision course was being set between the conservative norms that developed at the end of the war and the social movements that were gaining the attention of the young. Hollywood was in its Golden Age. It was against this backdrop that Ruth and Ruby Crawford quietly and diligently worked to rise within the ranks of the bank, while at the same time being considered two of the most social and sociable ladies in Atlanta.

Chapter Eight

The Sixties

A young lady from the age of one to fourteen needs good parents; and after fourteen she needs good looks; and after forty, it's cash, cold cash.

—Ruby Crawford

For everyone in America, and Ruth and Ruby were no exceptions, the 1960s was a time of tremendous change. The decade dawned with a presidential election that by a very narrow margin sent the youngest President in our history into the White House with his fashionable wife and darling children. As the decade opened, the civil rights decisions of the Supreme Court from the 1950s were beginning to have deep and lasting effects. In that period there was a shift of political thinking and process to colleges and students, and the movement began slowly building momentum and "forging consensus," the term popular in that day. Atlanta experienced peaceful sit-ins at Rich's Department Store, the Woolworth's lunch counter, and other establishments, by newly-energized young people from Morehouse, Spelman, and Morris Brown Colleges, and Clark and Atlanta Universities, all traditionally black schools.

In 1962, Ivan Allen, Jr. was elected Mayor of Atlanta running his 1961 mayoral campaign against Lester Maddox, who before the decade was over would himself be propelled into the national spotlight and prove prominent in Atlanta and Georgia political and social history and the shaping of both. As the city and state worked their way through the civil rights issues confronting all of America, Mayor Allen represented a movement away from the segregationist policies that had become endemic to state politics and government in Georgia. He took on and continued William B. Hartsfield's legacy of a "city too busy to hate," and he presided over the office of mayor until the end of the turbulent decade. He is quoted as saying, "I learned there was no middle ground in civil rights."

Allen, along with many others, held Atlanta together through tragedy and the turmoil of the Civil Rights Movement that engulfed the rest of the South and America. And, it is important to this story and interesting to note that all three men, Hartsfield, Maddox, and Allen, men of disparate and divergent political viewpoints, were all very good friends of Ruth and Ruby Crawford.

A 1933 graduate of Georgia Tech, Mayor Allen was warmly known as "Ivie, Jr." He followed his father's lead as a prominent and productive citizen of Atlanta. Ivan Allen, Sr. had a long legacy of commercial accomplishment and community improvement in the form of his "Forward Atlanta" campaign in the 1920s, upon which his son built.

"We just loved Mayor Allen. He did so much for the city," Ruby remembered. "He was one of our favorites."

"He was one of the nicest men, and one of the best mayors Atlanta ever had," Ruth added. "We loved his father, too. He was a fine man, who really loved Atlanta, our adopted home."

When Ivan Allen, Jr. was sworn in as Mayor of Atlanta in January 1962, public institutions of learning at all levels in Atlanta and throughout Georgia began to be desegregated peacefully. Hamilton Holmes and Charlayne Hunter became the first black students enrolled at the University of Georgia. Shortly after that, graduate student Mary Frances Early in 1962 became the first African-American to be awarded a degree from UGA when she earned her Master's Degree in music education. In 1963, Ms. Hunter and Mr. Holmes each earned undergraduate degrees.

During the Civil Rights Movement, Atlanta and all of Georgia stand out as unique in that era. In contrast to Birmingham, Selma, Montgomery, Little Rock in the South—northern and western cities of Boston, Los Angeles, Chicago, Detroit, and Washington, D.C.—Atlanta avoided the violence that plagued those places. Early in the civil rights debate, due in very large measure to Mayor Allen and before him Mayor Hartsfield, along with the black leadership in the city, John Wesley Dobbs among them, dialog opened between the emerging black leadership and the established white leadership. Those cooperative efforts allowed for peaceable solutions rather than contentious or violent ones. Having set a tone for peaceful transition rather than the combative posture adopted by so many other American cities, Atlanta made changes without the rancor and hostility the country had come to expect. That does not mean there was not tension; there was. But the city did not explode.

In the early 60s, Ruth and Ruby Crawford were moving up in the bank, though not at a pace that their prodigious energy, talent, and work ethic should have yielded. But those were the times, and civil rights inequities were not confined to those of African heritage; they extended to women on a very large scale. The pervasive "glass ceiling" was firmly in place, its full force and effect existing not only for those whose ethnicity set them apart, but for those whose gender did as well.

"I was admitted to practice before the Supreme Court of the United States before the bank made me an officer," Ruby remembers. "And they were none too quick about it even then. I think it took them about two years to do it. Finally, I became an officer. Before then, we got all kinds of publicity. The papers would carry my picture, and I'd say that I wanted to be an officer of the bank, but, you know what they say 'the prophet is without honor in his own country.' We felt like that many times, but we just kept doing what we were doing, believing that it would get better for us, and for others."

"Jack Flynt was my Congressman. He was the one who moved for my admission to the Supreme Court. I had asked Senator Herman Talmadge if he would move for my admission, but Senator Talmadge just spit in the cuspidor he had in his office and said, 'Ruby, I can't move your admission,' and I said 'Well, why not?' He said, 'I have not been admitted to that august body.' He didn't think too much of the Supreme Court. That was the time when Earl Warren was Chief Justice, when there were 'Impeach Earl Warren' signs all over the South. There were a lot of people who were upset with Justice Warren."

Of great benefit to the bank, and to the careers of Ruth and Ruby, was the steady flow of good publicity generated by the Crawford sisters' accomplishments. Their achievements and their character, drive, flair, and devotion to community issues, coupled with their loyalty to their employer, made them wonderful and quite often free or very inexpensive spokespersons for the bank, not just in Atlanta, but everywhere they went. It was not uncommon for the Crawford sisters to appear in newspapers in Pittsburgh, Dallas, New York, Chicago, and other cities. Much of the travel the Crawford sisters did on behalf of the bank was at their own expense.

—

> While men get their pictures on money,
> women get their hands on it,
> and that's what really counts.

"We looked at that as an investment in ourselves. It was good for people to see women in the roles we were in. We felt very fortunate to be there. So we didn't make much fuss about that kind of thing," Ruth noted.

In the years following the hard-earned promotions of Ruth and Ruby Crawford to officers in First Atlanta Bank, other women in Georgia began to find their way to officer status in the state's banking institutions. Columbus Bank and Trust Company (now part of Synovus), the venerable institution in that city, promoted Jackie Floyd to the officer level in the Proofs Department and Eleanor Carden to assistant branch manager in 1967. Mary Alice Maddox followed shortly thereafter from the Bookkeeping Department and was promoted to bank officer before the end of the decade. Jackie Floyd recalls, "When we retired, we were all vice-presidents." Ruth and Ruby had made it not "unheard of" for a woman to become an officer of a bank.

In 1962, a few months after Mayor Allen took office, Atlanta was rocked like no other city in America when on June 3 the horrifying news reached the city that a Boeing jet carrying civic leaders and members of Atlanta's arts community had crashed at Orly Airport in Paris. The passengers were returning home from a tour of European museums sponsored by the Atlanta Art Association as part of an effort to bring arts to a more prominent place in Atlanta. There were only two survivors. One hundred and twenty-two passengers and eight crew members died. One hundred and six were from Atlanta. Among those lost were the artists and community leaders who made up a great part of the arts community in Atlanta and Georgia. The sisters' dear friend, Mayor Ivan Allen, traveled to France without delay to assist with the recovery, immediately distinguishing himself in that tragic situation.

"Ruby and I," Ruth remembered, "were scheduled to go on that trip, but we were hosting the American Institute of Banking's Annual Convention in Atlanta for banking people from all over and our duties kept us here."

"We were chilled to the bone when we got the news. Many of our friends were on that plane."

"We lost a lot of close friends on that trip. Atlanta has never been quite the same since."

"Mayor Allen was wonderful in that very terrible situation. All those young children. It was just a very bad time here." Thirty-three children, from toddlers to teenagers to young adults, lost both parents in the tragedy.

Out of the ashes of the Orly catastrophe, the Art Association became the Atlanta Arts Alliance and went on to operate the High Museum, the Atlanta

Symphony, the Alliance Theater, the 14th Street Playhouse, and the Atlanta College of Art. On June 3, 1966, ground was broken for the Atlanta Memorial Arts Center. It opened in 1968, and a casting of Auguste Rodin's *The Shade (L'Ombre)* was presented to the city by the French government as a memorial to the victims of the Orly crash.

As Atlanta continued to grow, the Crawford women watched and participated in the progress as Mayor Allen presided over the beginnngs of The Woodruff Arts Center and the building of Atlanta-Fulton County Stadium, first home of the Atlanta Braves baseball team. The following year the city gained a professional football franchise when Rankin Smith, Sr. bought the Falcons expansion franchise from the National Football League. Construction started on the Atlanta Civic Center and on Interstate 285, better known to residents as the Perimeter. At the confluence of Interstates 75 and 85 in downtown Atlanta the Connector was built and continues to receive facelifts every few years as growth and traffic dictate.

It is cliché, though nonetheless true, that few Americans who were alive and aware of the world at the time will forget where they were on November 22, 1963 when President John F. Kennedy was assassinated. Vice-President Lyndon Johnson, from Texas, was sworn in aboard Air Force One as it was preparing for take-off to transport the President's body back to Washington. Newspapers all over the world ran the photograph of the President's widow, Jacqueline Bouvier Kennedy, standing beside Johnson as U. S. District Court Judge Sarah Hughes, a friend of the Crawford sisters, administered the oath of office.

"We were," the sisters agreed, "just like everybody in the country, devastated by President Kennedy's death. It was such a tragedy. He was so young, and those young children. It was not a good time."

Carl Edward Sanders was Governor of Georgia, inaugurated in January of 1963. Sanders was a change from what had become the status quo among

Georgia governors in that he was from an urban area, something that Georgia's governor had not been since the Twenties, and he was the first modern Georgia governor elected by popular vote, after the County Unit System[16] was declared unconstitutional.

Governor Sanders improved Georgia's educational system at all levels and began to institute environmental measures well before the environment was as politically and socially sensitive an issue as it is today. Known as Georgia's "good roads" governor, Sanders pushed through many significant changes to enhance transportation throughout the state.

For the Crawford sisters, business continued pretty much as usual at the bank, but against the backdrop of the monumental changes unfolding in Atlanta, across Georgia, and throughout the country. They continued to work and to reap the benefits that work provided, but in a much more limited way than the men with whom they worked. It is important to note that there were provisions in the Civil Rights Act that would eventually make things better for women in the workplace. But as of the mid-to-late 1960s that area of the law had not been tested in the courts to the degree that the race issues had been. While the Civil Rights Movement produced vast changes for people of color, the Women's Movement neither enjoyed the same level of passion and momentum nor an equivalent level of attention by the nation's courts, including its highest court.

In addition, for many women, especially Southern women, Ruth and Ruby among them, the Women's Movement had little personal appeal. What mattered to them was doing a good job, consistently, and for the long haul, in the confident hope that at some point people would begin to take notice, putting them on a level playing field with everyone else.

"While we believed that women should be treated equally in employment matters, salaries, promotions, and that sort of thing, but we were not protesters," Ruth remarked.

"And, we wanted to make whatever we made on our own, through our own efforts," Ruby added, "not simply because we happen to be women. Or because we made noise, called attention to ourselves. There was, or at least it seemed to us there was, a lot of that sort of thing in any 'movement.' We just wanted to do our jobs to the best of our ability and not have our gender make any difference at all."

Ironically, many business writers have observed that it was just this "get along and do a good job" attitude that helped perpetuate the glass ceiling; that is, men tended to call attention to their achievements, and when they did, good things happened. Whereas, women tended to let their work speak for itself and assume that it would be noticed and rewarded. In many circles, this has proven to be the overland rather than the express route to success.

While some change would eventually take place in the coming decades, in that era legal matters involving women were not addressed to any great degree. Granted, there began to be a great deal of media attention on the subject, but little of substantive effect took place in the '60s. That would take more time.

As the decade drew to a close, there was a new governor in Georgia. The Atlanta-born son of a steelworker, Lester Maddox, rose to the highest office in the state in 1967. In his early political career, Governor Maddox was a bit of a throwback for a time, given his views on desegregation that he at one time vigorously opposed. His view changed and moderated as the political and social landscape transformed.

"Governor Maddox was our dear, dear friend," Ruth and Ruby recalled, "and we did so many things for him, especially after his wife Virginia died. He was so appreciative of the attention that we gave him. One time we took him a whole basket of food, enough to last him for a week. We had baked him an apple pie with pecan praline topping. By the time we got from his house back to our house the phone was ringing. It was Governor Maddox. He said, 'I want you to know that you can't buy a piece of pie that delicious in the city of Atlanta for $100 in any hotel in town.' He was so appreciative, and he never minded telling you so."

Lester Maddox drew national attention in his response to the Civil Rights Act of 1964 and his willingness to sell his Pickrick Restaurant, famous for its skillet-fried chicken, where he and his family were employed. Later, Governor Maddox's popular and successful efforts on behalf of Georgians included pay increases for teachers, money for schools, and softened views on race that led to his appointing more black Georgians to state posts than any other governor before him; the first African-American to head a state department, the Board of Corrections; the first black GBI agent; and the first black State Trooper. Even farmers' markets, rarely thought of as racial battlegrounds though nonetheless "separate but equal," were peacefully integrated on his watch.

In his later years, every morning outside his modest home near the intersection of Johnson Ferry and Shallowford Roads in Cobb County, where Ruth and Ruby were frequent visitors, Governor Maddox could be found waving good morning to every commuter who passed that intersection. On the sixty-first anniversary of his marriage to his beloved Virginia, nee Virginia Cox, the Governor erected a hand-painted sign thanking God for her and for their life together. The sign read "Thanks be to God; He has given me my precious Virginia for 61 years as of May 9, '97." When Virginia passed away shortly thereafter, the Governor put up a second sign that read: "and God took her from me and carried her home 45 days later."

Overall, his was not a bad legacy for a man who had to drop out of school as a teenager to help support the family, who started a restaurant with his wife and kids and their last $400, and who later rode his bicycle to work at the State Capital, being "green" before his time. This was a man who appreciated a good piece of pie and who could claim Ruth and Ruby Crawford among his closest friends.

Chapter Nine

Dogs, Dogs, Dogs, Dogs, Dogs

Dogs are not our whole life, but they make our lives whole.

—Roger Caras
President of the ASPCA (1991–1999)

"Our little ol' daddy had hunting dogs when we were growing up, bird dogs and hounds, that sort of thing," Ruth recalled. "And we loved every one of them. We'd roll our doll carriages up and down the street, and if anyone had puppies, we'd put the dolls out and put the puppies in and roll them up and down the street. We've always loved dogs."

"Over the years we have had lots of dogs," Ruby continued. "We had the three poodles, Celebrity, Sweetheart, and Sugar Boy. All told, we've had thirteen dogs. The poodles were the last ones."

"Celebrity was the one who had clearance to the White House. We inherited him from a man at Jekyll Island who had passed away. He was about seven years old when we got him. He went everywhere with us whenever he could. He campaigned for President Carter. We took him on all the trips where we could drive. When we had chartered planes like going up to New Hampshire and Vermont, then Celebrity couldn't go. Ruth stayed with him and worked at the headquarters. In Tennessee, Florida, Georgia, and the surrounding states, where we could drive, we took Celebrity, so he wore the green and white colors of the campaign. He had a pretty little green coat with white fur and we put stickers on his pretty little long hairy ears that said Carter-Mondale. He was on television a lot, too."

"We used to take them with us to the Peachtree, you know, the Road Race, every year."

"Our little doggies just loved it. They'd get so excited. Now people say 'Where are the poodles?'"

"We love dogs. We always have. Growing up, we always had all kinds of them, every shape and size. It didn't make any difference to us, we loved them all."

"When we were working years ago," Ruby said, "we had our little doggies, and Daddy and Mama kept our 'babies' during the week. We were at the bank during the day and going to school at night and we just couldn't keep our little doggies over here in Atlanta with us. So, they kept the babies."

"Kept the 'grandchildren,' you might say," Ruth added.

"After Celebrity," the poodle who helped elect Jimmy Carter, "we had two other dogs. We went to the same kennel where Celebrity was born. He was such a fine dog. His maternal and paternal grandparents and parents were champion dogs. We drove six hundred miles up to Delaware to the Round Table Kennels."

"The lady who owned it had won all kinds of awards and trophies from all over the world for her dogs. The big dog had puppies, seven little darling poodle puppies, and we drove up, and it took us from Sunday to Monday afternoon to decide which two to take, because we wanted to take all of them, and we should have."

"We adopted two of them and brought them home with us. The kennel people gave us carrying cages, put them in the car with our little dogs in each one. But that didn't last any time at all. By the time we left the place we had one on each of our shoulders as we shared the driving home. They were such good dogs that we didn't have to put them in the cage at all the whole way back to Atlanta."

"So we spent the night in Salisbury, North Carolina, and the next morning we went to McDonald's, which was adjacent to the motel, and our little doggies had their first Egg McMuffins. When we got back home, we shipped the carrying cases back to the lady at the kennel. Those dogs simply didn't need them. Their maternal grandfather was international champion and the father was a national champion poodle, so we were kind of spoiled about having fine little poodles."

"They were with us for fifteen years. Another dog we had lived to be nineteen years old and we hoped these would too, but we lost little Sweetheart. At first we called them Piddles and Puddles, because at the time that was the appropriate name for them, and then we felt they needed more mature names so we named them Kandi and Kisses, but later we called them Sweetheart and Sugar Boy."

"Mayor Hartsfield's wife said, 'Ruth and Ruby, that's the cutest thing you all have ever done, having little twin poodles. What are you going to call them?' and I said, 'Well, it doesn't matter what name we give them because we'll just call them names like Sweetheart and Honey Boy and Sugar Love and anything else we can think of. They probably won't ever hear their real names as far as we're concerned.' So they were named Kandi and Kisses. Little Sweetheart, the one we thought was the healthiest, died of a heart condition. We knew he wasn't feeling well and we took him to his doctor. He said, 'I'm just giving you medicine for about three days,' and I said, 'Oh, don't tell me that we're going to lose our baby.' But we did."

The ladies buried their beloved pets in little caskets from the H. M. Patterson Funeral Directors. "We bought a cherub casket for each one of ours. Spring Hill was so nice as to offer to come and dig the grave and put them in the casket for us, but we said, 'Thank you so much, but we'll ask our yard man to do it.'"

"And we did. We buried all of our dogs out in our rose garden. They were such fine little babies. We looked for a long time for twin poodles to replace the ones we had who went to Heaven. We kept looking for replacements at the Humane Society. We would have gone back to the same kennels, but that was the last breeding. The lady was ninety-four years old then, and she couldn't get anybody to take over her kennels and so she was going out of business. So we couldn't have gotten any more from the same kennel, or we would have gone immediately and gotten more. We just never did find any we wanted."

"Now, we are godparents to poodles down in Longwood, Florida. They send us cards saying 'Guess who went out to buy this Mother's Day card' and on the inside, 'Your cute little godchild, that's who.' So we love other people's dogs. We love to start talking about our babies. They really were like our children. We took them every place. We bought a van so we could all travel together. We were never happier than 'Us Four and No More" –the two of them and the two of us."

"It's one of those GM Explorer vans with rose-colored upholstery and a television."

"We had it custom made."

"For the dogs. Well, truth be told, for all of us."

"We loved it. Little Sweetheart would sit on the sofa, and the chairs, and up front. But little Sugar Boy didn't want anybody to get where we were going before he did, so he'd stick to that front seat, right up there with the driver. He didn't wander around in the van. He would occasionally, but most of the time he stuck to his seat. But Little Sweetheart would wander all over the van. We just enjoyed those trips so much."

"We traveled all over the place."

"We went to Lansing, Michigan to the International Twin Convention, to Washington, D.C., up through New York and over to Chicago. We just traveled and traveled with our little dogs."

"We're members of the International Twin Convention. For a while, we went every year, unless it was some city we didn't particularly care for. It's Labor Day weekend every year."

"Mayor Hartsfield said that the next best thing to going to Heaven was being one of the Crawfords' dogs. And the Mayor of Temple used to say, 'When they're talking about leading a dog's life, they're not talking about the Crawfords' dogs.'"

Chapter Ten

Matters of Taste and Entertainment

It's difficult to think anything but pleasant thoughts while eating a homegrown tomato.

—Lewis Grizzard

"We love to eat," Ruth happily confesses. "I've always told everyone I never wanted to die indebted to my stomach."

"I'm a meat and potatoes gal," Ruby says. "I'm not overly fond of too many herbs and spices and things, but there are some things I just couldn't cook without, like broiled steak seasoning and lemon pepper and garlic. Those are my favorites. Steak is my favorite food. If there's anything better, I've never discovered it. I like steaks and roast beef and prime rib and all that. And I like it rare. I want it to moo at me when it comes out. I just want the body heat restored."

"We like pork, lamb, and chicken, too," Ruth adds. "We've been chicken-eating Methodists all our lives. I've loved fried chicken all my life, but now I don't choose chicken quite so much. We lean more toward seafood since we've been going to the coast so much, shrimp and lobster. Lobster is my favorite."

"Steak and lobster on the same plate wouldn't offend me," Ruby continues. "That's my choice. Surf and turf. I really like Southern food better than any kind of cooking, French or Italian or Mexican."

Ruth recalled, "I'm a little more champagne and caviar than Ruby. I really enjoy a glass of good champagne."

Such eclectic tastes are not limited to champagne, caviar, or steak and potatoes. In their interview with Dr. Betty Siegel on Kennesaw State University's Meet the President, the Crawford sisters reminisced about their indulgences, one of which is a regular visit to The Varsity, the Atlanta drive-in founded by Frank Gordy.

Ruby related that, "We know the Gordys quite well. This year (2008) was the eightieth anniversary of The Varsity. Mrs. Gordy liked some of the stories we had told her and she had us include some of them in the book they were writing about The Varsity for their seventy-fifth anniversary a few years ago. So I wrote two of the stories. One of them concerned our late beloved Mayor Hartsfield. He and Tollie, his wife, and son Carl used to love to go to The Varsity to eat, as did many other hundreds and thousands of people, I guess. Many afternoons when Tollie would go over to pick up the mayor, they would come back to The Varsity and have a hot dog. When the prices were raised from ten cents to two for fifteen cents to two for a quarter and then to a quarter, Mayor Hartsfield said that, 'If they keep raising those prices at The Varsity, they're going to drive us back to the Capital City Club.'"

Ruth laughed when she recalled that when the new First National Bank building was under construction the bank employees were "farmed out to other office buildings" all over the city. Ruby's temporary office was "down at North Avenue only a couple of blocks from The Varsity. So she'd go down and eat her hot dogs and things at lunch and then she would get me mine down through either the [bank's] courier or Brink's, you know, in a big brown manila envelope to number 10 Pryor Street where I was. So she would send me my lunch. Of course, everyone thought they were hauling securities, or bonds, or stocks. But it was very valuable."

"I sealed them up," Ruby adds, "in a heavy brown envelope, very securely, so they couldn't smell the onion rings and all the hot dogs and the chili, and then I would send them by the first available courier, the porter, or Brink's or whatever, whoever was going first to Ruth. They thought they were hauling something very valuable, but we knew it wasn't stocks and bonds; it was just Varsity hot dogs."

Ruth and Ruby love food and pride themselves on eating nearly everything. "We have zero tolerance for finicky eaters, and even less for their children. We grew up in an era when you ate what was put in front of you, and you were glad to have it."

"When we were little. Daddy and our brother would go hunting all the time," Ruth remembered, "We'd have just about anything you can think of. It wasn't unusual for us to have rabbit, squirrel, venison, a wild turkey, you name it and we probably had it. And we'd have whatever kinds of vegetables we grew, greens, beans, potatoes, okra, corn, tomatoes, just about anything."

Ruby adds "There's nothing that I won't eat. I guess the only thing I've never eaten is rattlesnake. I've eaten alligator but never rattlesnake. But if I were offered rattlesnake, I'd give it a try."

Anyone with less prodigious energy than Ruth and Ruby might wonder: With all they had to do professionally, as well as their civic and church activities, and all the cooking and entertaining they have done over the years, and the travel, politics, and various and sundry other activities, how in the world would Ruth and Ruby have had time to do anything else? But with these two, there was more.

"We had all sorts of hobbies," Ruth recalled.

"There wasn't anything we didn't like, except bridge. We felt that every minute we spent playing bridge was time wasted in our lives," Ruby added.

"Now we don't mean to offend anyone by saying this," Ruth explained. "We have lots of friends who play bridge, but it was just not to our taste."

—

When I'm asked why I am not married,
I reply that I have a chimney that smokes,
a dog that barks, howls, and growls, a parrot that
swears, and a cat that stays out all night.
So why do I need a husband?

"I think it's because to play bridge well, we have to sit still too long, and we like to see something tangible for the time we spend doing something."

"Our hobbies were doggies, first of all. We loved our little dogs."

"Flower gardening and cooking was my favorite thing to do. Cooking has never been a chore to me. It's just relaxation. I've never been too tired to cook in my life. I love to fix food and have other people enjoy it.

Of course, we were also musical. We studied piano and voice."

"We sang primarily hymns, sang in the glee club," Ruth remembered. "We used to play the piano at church, and we sang in the choir. We love music. We've gone to the musicals for years, the All-Star Concert Series. We love operas and classical, but we like music played and sung like it's written."

"We've even been in movies and on television ourselves."

"In 1954, we were on *What's My Line?*[17] and we stumped the panel. Of course, John Daly was the MC. A few years ago, some friends of ours sent for the tape of that show and asked us over for dinner. They surprised us and played the tape of our appearance. I was shocked to death. On that show there was Dorothy Kilgallen, Arlene Francis, Bennett Cerf, Robert Q. Lewis and, of course, John Daly. Merle Oberon, the actress, was on that show as well. They always had a star, and Miss Oberon was the movie star on the night that we appeared. At that time we were the only twin-women-lawyer members of the American Bar Association. So we stumped the panel. Bennett Cerf thought one of us was Coca and the other was Cola, being from Atlanta. Dorothy Kilgallen thought we demonstrated twin egg beaters and Arlene Francis thought that we played twin pianos, and I can't think what Robert Q. Lewis thought we did, but he missed it, too. Anyway, it was a delight to appear on that show."

"In 2000, we were on *Oprah*, which was great fun. And we've been written about in Maryln Schwartz's book *A Southern Belle Primer or Why Princess Margaret Will Never Be A Kappa Kappa Gamma*. That picture of us on page 26, with Miss Georgia, was taken at a meeting of the Gracious Ladies of Georgia."

"We were also in a movie, made down at Jekyll Island, where we have a place and where we have gone for years. The movie was called *Jekyll–No Place to Hyde* and we had supporting roles. We also did all those programs for the American bankers in Washington, New York, New Orleans, San Diego, Mexico, and all sorts of other places. When the American Bankers decided they would do their own PR program, they elected Ruth and me to represent women in banking all over the United States."

"In 1994," Ruby recalls, "we were extras in the movie the *Oldest Living Confederate Widow Tells All*. It was great fun. We were in that scene where they're carrying the widow out of the house to an ambulance. The director had us all standing around there and he told us, 'Now this lady's sick, so everyone should look concerned for her,' and then the scene started. Well, for some reason he didn't like that scene and he called for another take, and then another, and another. It was hot out there and the director must have called for about eleven takes. On the last take we were all just miserable, feeling like we were being roasted alive, so we looked even more glum. The director scolded us, saying, 'She's just sick, she's not dead.' Well, I piped up and said, 'She soon will be if we don't finish this scene.'"

"We loved to entertain. Putting on a big affair was one of our favorite things," Ruth remembered. "We'd do all the cooking, the decorating, the hosting, and the cleanup afterward. It was something that we really enjoyed, having a group of people to our home to enjoy themselves; that was one of our greatest pleasures."

"We studied all kinds of things, from ceramics to oil painting to china painting. Music and the arts are things that we really enjoy. We learned flower gardening from the time we were children, and everywhere we have ever lived we have had flowers in the yard."

"I can't imagine living any place where we didn't have at least a few flowers."

"I love to fish," Ruby states emphatically. "Ruth would always tell everyone, 'If you want to get home before dark, don't go fishing with Ruby.' I like to catch any kind that will bite my hook, but I especially like fishing for trout and flounder down at Jekyll. Ruth didn't fish so much, but she was good at minding the crab traps. But I've fished in Florida and Tennessee. I use a fly rod and I have been known to make my own flies."

"Our daddy would put three fish hooks at different intervals. Sometimes he would come up with a little trout on each hook, three at a time. One time up at Gatlinburg we went fishing out at Douglas Dam. I never saw the fish bite so fast in all my life. We just thought we had the finest string of fish. Ruth and I had to quit fishing to string Daddy's up. We wanted him to be the one to catch the fish because he was having such a good time doing it. When we got back to our motel with that long string of fish, we were going to cook them and the lady who owned the motel said, 'Oh, you can't eat those. They came out of Douglas Dam. There's kerosene in that lake and the fish will taste like kerosene.' So we couldn't eat our fish."

"We've been going fishing since we were children. But we kept it up even after we were grown. We used to fish on the creek banks out at Temple. That was the place that we had to fish then. Mother and Daddy loved to fish. There were a few large creeks and they'd catch carp. That's kind of a strong-tasting fish, but if you just remove the skin from the carp, you had good fish. We caught crawfish and would take the shell off and fry them up. They were like little shrimp."

"Whenever we had a catch, I'd skin 'em and Daddy would gut 'em. Daddy and I had ourselves a pretty good little fish cleaning business going on there."

"We used to take Daddy and Mother every Saturday up to Lake Allatoona, and we'd fix fried chicken and stuffed eggs and pimento cheese sandwiches and potato salad. Ruth would cast out her line and get her chair, get the dog up in her lap, turn the radio on, and get her book open, and wait for lunch. She was a real serious fisherman," Ruby laughs. "Ruth didn't care whether they bit or not, but I was there to catch fish. And there would be Ruth with the radio beside her, the dog in her lap, her book opened, and her line out waiting for me to tell her lunch was ready. Ruth wasn't much for fishing, but she did like lunch. We always had such a great time. Mother and Daddy loved doing that. And Ruth did, too."

"And, sure enough," Ruby says, "Ruth was right. We didn't get home before dark."

Chapter Eleven

Things Political

Ruth and Ruby Crawford have been friends and supporters of mine for many years and were a mainstay of the Peanut Brigade in 1976. They are remarkable women who achieved success and respect in business during a time when this was uncommon for women. They continue to brighten any occasion with their wit, intelligence, and colorful matching dress. They are great supporters of many worthwhile causes and are a valuable resource for Georgia.

—President Jimmy Carter

We just couldn't wait to become old enough to vote. At that time, we had to wait until we were twenty-one years of age. After Vietnam all that changed, and now people vote at eighteen. We would have loved to have been able to vote at eighteen, but we had to wait despite the fact that we were active in politics."

"Neither of us ever ran for any office, but we were both very interested in politics all our lives, from age thirteen on, and we still are."

Ruth added, "I was tempted to run. Kind of. I thought about running for representative from Carroll County, but I didn't feel like I would be able to spend all the time out there that would be required to be a good representative—something I would have had to do if I were in office—and do what I had to do here in Atlanta, too. As much as I love my hometown, I also loved Atlanta and wanted to be here."

Politics in America took another ugly turn in 1968 when Robert F. Kennedy, younger brother of the assassinated President, was gunned down in Los Angeles while campaigning for the Democratic nomination. Civil rights leader Martin Luther King, Jr. was shot on the balcony outside his room in the Lorraine Motel in Memphis while on his way to supper. The United States coped poorly when Detroit, Washington, D.C., Los Angeles, and Chicago began to explode in response to those tragic events making the Spring and Summer of 1968 one of the most unsettled periods in American social and political history. That Fall, Richard Nixon was elected president in a very close contest against Hubert Humphrey, Johnson's Vice-President. Student unrest filled the headlines and disrupted college campuses all over the country. The decade of the Sixties closed not with the proverbial whimper, but with a bang, and a rather loud one at that.

When James Earl Carter, Jr., from Plains, Georgia, announced his candidacy for President of the United States in December of 1974, he began a two-year campaign that started slowly but eventually gained enough momentum to propel him into the White House. People from all over the country, including Ruth and Ruby Crawford, worked as volunteers on a campaign that saw Jimmy Carter nominated on the first ballot at the Democratic National Convention that Summer. Ruth was elected as a delegate to the convention in New York.

President Carter had been Governor of Georgia from 1971 until 1974. He also served two terms in the Georgia Senate. A graduate of the U. S. Naval Academy, President Carter was former Naval Officer whose roots run deep and long in Georgia soil. James Earl "Jimmy" Carter, Jr., a self-styled "Washington outsider," became the thirty-ninth Chief Executive, occupying the office from 1977 to 1981.

"Ruth and I had just retired from the bank when Jimmy made his announcement that he was going to run. We had always admired him, and we said if he's going to run for President, then we're going to help him all we can. So we started working here in the Atlanta headquarters first, and soon we were going on campaign trips for him."

"When we could drive, we drove the car. For other places we flew. Ruth didn't like to fly anyway, so she usually stayed home and kept the poodles and worked in the headquarters. On one trip, I spent seventeen days in Vermont and New Hampshire. During that trip, they, the people at headquarters, called up there and asked, 'Would you go to Oklahoma and Texas when you get back?' and I said, 'Well, I'll be happy to, if you'll give me a chance to get my shoes half-soled!'"

Recalling the rigors of winter in the Northeast, Ruby muses, "We worked in snow, sleet, and ice. I wonder why we didn't break our necks. Going from house to house, door to door, telling people about President Carter, giving them the literature and telling them that we were there at our own expense, working as volunteers for him, and people would say, 'Jimmy who?' They didn't know a lot about him then, so we would tell them about what a fine person of integrity and intelligence he was and why we wanted him to be the President and why we thought he would make a good President."

"We went to stores and shopping centers, and as people went in and out of the grocery stores, we were there to hand out literature. House to house, political rallies, football games, radio and television, meetings at city halls, everything you can think of. Wherever they were having a crowd, we showed up in town. It was great. We met a lot of wonderful people."

"We covered New Hampshire and all the New England states, plus Oklahoma, Texas, Missouri, St. Louis, especially, and Florida, South Carolina, Tennessee, and Georgia, just all over the place."

"I don't recall whether I ever did get those shoes half-soled. But I did leave one pair under a lawyer's bed up in New Hampshire. What was so funny about it was I was in Manchester, New Hampshire, three different times, and I was to stay with a couple. We got off the plane and went to the Carter headquarters and everybody was farmed out to various houses. The local people were so gracious to let us stay in their homes like that. When they came to pick me up, they asked if I would like to go to a Christmas party, and I said, 'Thank you, I'd love to, but you all just go ahead and go. I need to make some telephone calls.'"

"Well, don't you know, the next morning there was a tap on my door and my host asked, 'Do you like bacon and eggs for breakfast?' and I said, 'Yes, I'm getting dressed and I'll be out to help fix breakfast shortly.' When I came out, I didn't see anybody but this gentleman. I didn't see the lady of the house. Come to find out, she wasn't there. So it was just the two of us."

"Oh my, did our people kid me about that–spending the night alone with a lawyer in his house! I told them, 'I hate to admit this, but the only thing that crawled in the bed with me was that big sheep dog.' He felt so warm and soft and cuddly, and I was missing my little dogs so much.'"

"And wouldn't you know that the only time that I wore boots up there was that morning. I put on my boots and forgot my shoes and left them under the bed. Well, when the people at headquarters found that out they really started kidding me–leaving my shoes and hoping to go back. That was quite a joke. I don't think I ever got those shoes back."

"We met great people, all the mayors of the towns we visited and Senator Pat Leahy. They even got to kidding me about him. He met our plane when we landed in Burlington, Vermont, and the front page of the paper showed a picture of Sen. Patrick Leahy and me under an umbrella."

"That day we reported to headquarters. We then drove down to Rutledge, Vermont and we made the front page there, so I was on the front page of two papers in one day. We just had a great time with the mayor and the governor. At one of the banquets Senator Leahy came by and kissed me goodbye when he started to leave, and they really did start kidding me about him because he paid so much attention to me. So every time he comes on television Ruth will say, 'Oh, Ruby, here's your boyfriend!' You know, he has a lot to say; he doesn't hesitate to say what he thinks about things. He's a great Senator. They love him dearly in Vermont. That was just the greatest experience, telling people about Jimmy."

On January 20, 1977, when President Jimmy Carter, using his full name, was inaugurated the thirty-ninth President of the United States, Ruth and Ruby Crawford were there and at the festivities held later that evening, the first group to be entertained at the White House by President and Mrs. Carter.

"I remember coming back from the Inauguration," Ruby says. "We all went up for that. Celebrity went because he had campaigned. That's when he was interviewed on NBC on the six o'clock news on Inauguration Day, our little poodle, Celebrity. You don't get any more prominent than being recognized at six o'clock on NBC! And they asked him what he thought about all those Democrats up there. Celebrity was just darling. He was so beautiful on the TV. He was just the most beautiful dog I've ever seen. Ruth used to say she hated to go to sleep at night and quit looking at him, he was so beautiful. And he was."

"Celebrity was very much a Democrat," Ruth would say. "I guess you could say he was a 'yellow dog' Democrat, except his fur was white."

"We, the Peanut Brigaders of which Ruth and I were members, were invited to five different functions at the White House in the first year of President Carter's administration."

By this time, Ruth and Ruby Crawford were as much fixtures in Atlanta as Coca-Cola and boiled peanuts. Their involvement in the life of the city and across the state of Georgia saw them at mayoral and gubernatorial functions, along with all of the other work to which they were devoted. George Busbee succeeded Jimmy Carter as Governor of Georgia. During that era, Sam Massell was elected in October 1969 as the first Jewish mayor in Atlanta history.

"We went to law school with Sam Massell," Ruby recalled. "We worked on the yearbook together. He's been our good buddy for years."

Mayor Massell's administration is credited with creating Atlanta's mass transit authority, MARTA, and building the Omni, the first enclosed coliseum in the city. Woodruff Park, named for Robert W. Woodruff, President of Coca-Cola from 1923 until 1954, opened in 1973. Mr. Woodruff purchased the land and donated to the city in 1971. The park is located in the heart of downtown Atlanta, between Edgewood Avenue, Peachtree Street, and Park Place, a place where only a few decades before Ruth and Ruby rode streetcars to and from the bank, law school, and home. There are two fountains there now, a pavilion, and several monuments, the most visible of which is the bronze sculpture of Phoenix Rising from the Ashes, symbolizing the city's rise from the fires of the Civil War.

In 1973, Maynard Holbrook Jackson, Jr., Mayor Massell's vice-mayor, defeated Massell in a runoff to become Atlanta's first black mayor. Mayor Jackson served three terms. One hundred and twenty-six years after its formal chartering as a city, Atlanta in 1974 had a mayor whose forebears had been in bondage when the first three mayors of Atlanta won their one-year terms

After a very eventful first term, President Carter stood for reelection in the 1980 presidential election. Ruby recalled, "Now the second time around they were telling us that people were not as receptive as they were in 1976. We worked both campaigns. It was the greatest experience. Sadly, we didn't make it the second time around."

Chapter Twelve

Investment
in Community

A nation, as a society, forms a moral person, and
every member of it is personally responsible for his
society.

—President Thomas Jefferson

When the twins retired from banking in 1974, they earned their real estate
licenses and became affiliated with Northside Realty Associates[18] in its
Buckhead office where they again made names for themselves. Among other
awards, Ruth and Ruby were named "Humanitarians of the Year" while at
the same time being inducted into the "Million Dollar Roundtable." Founded
in 1927, the MDRT recognizes real estate professionals who epitomize
successful sales ability and client service while maintaining the highest ethical
standards.

"It was in the real estate industry where we were finally paid on an equal
basis with men. It was the first and only time we enjoyed equal pay. We were
paid for what we did. There wasn't any issue between the pay of men and
women. You got what you earned."

The March 2002 issue of Atlanta Real Estate Executive carried the following
about Ruth and Ruby:

"It was recently announced that former Northside Realty
agents Ruth and Ruby Crawford will be inducted into the
next class of the Hall of Fame of the Atlanta Convention
and Visitors Bureau. The new class, to be inducted on
September 20th, will double the size of the current class
to eight members when it adds Ruth and Ruby, along with
other Atlanta notables Billy Payne and Ritz Carlton's Horst
Schultze. They join a short but elite list that includes Ted
Turner, Andrew Young and Tom Murphy.

They may not seem like household names like their
fellow Hall of Fame members, but in hospitality circles,

the Buckhead twins bear the unofficial title of "Atlanta's Goodwill Ambassadors to the World."

"I think of all the nice things we've had written and said about us, that is the nicest," Ruby observes. "To think that the people who know you say that about you. Well, it just made us so proud."

Not only were Ruth and Ruby known as trailblazers for women in the banking industry, they also blazed trails for women in the legal profession. Each served as President of the Georgia Association for Women Lawyers, and both were active in the legal profession for over sixty years. In 2006, GAWL named its endowment fund The Ruth and Ruby Crawford Scholarship Fund, and Ruby was awarded the organization's highest and most prestigious award given to a woman lawyer, The Kathleen Kessler Award.

Mayor Hartsfield often referred to Ruth and Ruby as "the twenty-four-hour Crawford twins." He also said of the sisters that "the reason Rome wasn't built in a day was because Ruth and Ruby weren't there."

The roster of organizations counting Ruth and Ruby Crawford as members is as distinguished as it is lengthy. Every organization that these remarkably energetic women joined could count on the fact that neither lady would join unless she believed in the cause and could make real contributions, giving of her time, industry, money, and that special Ruth-and-Ruby way of doing things, which has been likened to a force of nature. In 1967, Ruby was selected to appear in that year's edition of Outstanding Civic Leaders of America, in recognition of her outstanding ability, accomplishments, and service to community, country, and profession.

Ruby reflects, "Since 1974, I've been a member of the Board of Directors of the Atlanta Humane Society. And I am still a member. Just got elected for three more years. That will make thirty-five years I've been on the Board of Directors."

From the Board of Directors of the Atlanta Humane Society to the Gracious Ladies of Georgia and many stops in between, the Crawford sisters for over six decades have been icons of service and dedication, very active and effective icons, in civic affairs, community projects, charitable enterprises, and professional organizations in Atlanta, around the State of Georgia, and on the national stage. It is something in the blood, the way that they were brought up, the influence of William Hampton and Mary Elizabeth Crawford that instilled in them an unquenchable sense of duty and a desire to serve others.

In addition to their numerous activities, hobbies, civic pursuits, and service commitments, Ruth and Ruby also served on the Board of Directors of the Miss

Atlanta Beauty Pageant and as judges in numerous beauty pageants in other Georgia cities. In addition, the twins assisted their dear and good friend John Ferrell, Jr. when he took over as owner of the very popular Atlanta restaurant Mary Mac's Tea Room. Relying on their experience in the restaurant business from having done every job that needed doing in their father's restaurant when they were girls and young women, Ruth and Ruby served as hostesses, consulted on the menu, and Ruby "tested" all the dishes, critiquing the food, service, and atmosphere of the eatery. Their pictures adorn the walls in many places throughout Mary Mac's. The sisters explain that if the paint in Mary Mac's ever chips, they just put up another picture of Ruth and Ruby because it's cheaper than redecorating.

Recalling the many other organizations to which she and Ruth donated time, talent, and touch, Ruby remembers, "We've been in the Rotary Club for years. Every year at our home on Jekyll Island we would have a big Rotary Club function. We also had magazine food editors from time to time, and once we were visited by Better Homes and Gardens and Southern Living. All of them came down to Jekyll Island, Georgia and we hosted them at our house, fed them all, and bedded them down."

"I can't remember how many church groups we've hosted, but there have been a lot of them. Peachtree Road Methodist Church groups and Sandy Springs Sunday School class and St. Catherine's Choir from our church, those little twelve-to-fourteen-olds, came. There were eighteen of them, and we fed and bedded all of them down, too. They were so cute, thanking us for that wonderful weekend when we had them in our home. They just kept telling us what a great time they'd had and what wonderful hostesses we were. They'd say, 'We just want to thank you for having us in your beautiful house this weekend, and next year we'd like to come back and stay a week and a half.'"

"The STAR Students used to take a week-long trip around the state. They would start out in Atlanta, go to Six Flags and Stone Mountain, Georgia Tech, and Lockheed and all the other places of interest around the city. Then they would be off to Rome and Berry College and North Georgia and all the scenic attractions there. After that they were over in Augusta at the Medical College, and then they would travel down through Savannah and out to Tybee, St. Simon's Island, Sea Island, and Jekyll Island. Over to the Okefenokee Swamp and Waycross they'd go, and then head up to Abraham Baldwin and LaGrange Colleges. It was a wonderful trip for a week's time."

"The STAR Students of Georgia come from the best students in nearly every school in the state. The teachers and the STAR Students gather here from all over Georgia at the beginning of their trip and then again at the end.

I was fortunate enough to be in on the embryonic stages of setting up the STAR Student Recognition when I was on the Board of the Georgia Chamber of Commerce. When they reached Jekyll, we had them all come to the house for either lunch or dinner. They came on a Greyhound bus, and members the local Chamber of Commerce came along with them. One of our neighbors called one day after the bus had gone and said, 'Oh, did you live through it?' and we said, 'Of course we did. We had a great time.' And she said, 'I told my next door neighbor that the day a Greyhound bus drove up to my house I would go jump in the ocean, but I knew it wouldn't faze you all.' We said, 'Well, no. We're already cleaned up and ready for the next party.'"

Ruby remembers, "One of the things that was so great was that the STAR Students would write the loveliest notes about what a good time they had, and they voted every year on where they had the best food. Several times mine was voted the best food that they had on the whole trip. I felt that when we nosed out the Cloister that I had arrived in the world."

"The wonderful thing is going to those meetings every year with the STAR Students. These days some of the STAR teachers come up and say, 'I was at your house in 1968 as a STAR Student and now I have been chosen a STAR Teacher.' And it's such a thrill to see them now as STAR Teachers, after they had been STAR Students. Someone once asked us, 'When in the world are you going to quit doing all that?' and we said, 'It's not any trouble. We love fixing lunch and dinner for all those students, and they are such wonderful students and so appreciative and write such lovely notes about what a good time they had; so as long as they do that, we're going to continue to do this.'"

"These days, since the State shortened it to a weekend trip, they don't go down to the islands or all over the state any more. They restrict it to the Atlanta area. But it is still a wonderful experience for the students, the teachers, and everyone else participating in it."

"Usually there were about fifty or so, a busload. And some of the local representatives. We'd have about fifty-six or fifty-eight, and we did all the cooking, Ruth and I. And all the preparing. We had a great time–loved it."

"Oh and then there's the Rotary Club. We would have a continuous cocktail party and buffet when they had the meeting in Jekyll for the North Georgia group, the Buckhead Rotarians, and Rotarians from Bremen, Carrollton, and LaGrange. We know the people so well, so we had the party and reception from 1:00 in the afternoon until the president's reception at 6:00 in the evening. So whatever time someone arrived they could come, eat, and enjoy themselves. We did all the food for that, too. And it wasn't hot dogs and hamburgers; it was a spread, a real feast. We made all sorts of things: filet of beef, ham, a turkey breast, and all the things you could have for a buffet, including salads and casseroles and desserts."

"Every year on New Year's Day we would have a continuous open house and we had all those good old Southern dishes, you know. Usually there were three or four or even more meats: country fried steak, pork, chicken, chicken and dumplings, pot roast, collard greens and turnip greens, sweet potato souffle, and black-eyed peas, of course, along with salads, desserts, and all the trimmings. Recently one of the ladies down on Jekyll who used to never miss our party told me, 'I do wish you would get back to having your annual New Year's Day parties. We've missed them every year.' I'll tell you this, if somebody left one of those New Year's Day parties hungry, it was their own fault."

"We belonged, first of all, to the Women's Chamber of Commerce because the men wouldn't let us belong to theirs. Women could not belong to the Atlanta or to the Georgia Chambers of Commerce, so in 1937 women formed their own Chamber of Commerce, primarily devoting time and attention to making Atlanta a cleaner and more beautiful city. It was 'clean up, fix up, paint up, and make Atlanta beautiful.' That was the main objective. We joined in 1940-something. The Women's Chamber is nearly eighty years old now. They still meet, but it's not like it used to be. I don't know whether it's going to be going out of existence or not. There really is no need for having a separate Chamber since women can now belong to the Atlanta and the Georgia Chambers."

Ruby recalls, "From there, we did a lot of things, holding offices in the Women's Chamber of Commerce. I was Parliamentarian and then was elected President of the Southeastern Conference of Women in Chambers of Commerce. We had our annual meeting and banquet in Little Rock, Arkansas. While we were there, as a courtesy, Gov. Orval Faubus commissioned me an Arkansas Traveler. At that time I was only the second woman to be commissioned an Arkansas Traveler. That's an ambassador of good will for the State of Arkansas. So I'm an ambassador of goodwill for the State of Arkansas."

"We also attended meetings of the U.S. Chamber of Commerce. Every year, Ruth and I helped host the Congressional dinner for the Georgia delegation. Then I was appointed, as a result of my work on the Southeastern Conference of Women in Chambers of Commerce, to the public affairs committee of the United States Chamber of Commerce. I served three years on that committee with forty-six corporate CEOs. I used to say that this could not be little old me from Temple, Georgia, up here with all these CEOs from General Motors, General Electric, U. S. Steel, Republic Steel, The Oakland Times, and Bill Knowland, Senator from California. Little old me from Temple, Georgia, sitting up there with all that bunch."

"And then I served three years on the subcommittee of Women in Public Affairs. That necessitated trips to Washington about every month and was quite an honor. I guess it was one of the greatest honors ever given to me."

"Now, I don't know whether it was a result of that or the publicity about the fact that I had been appointed to that Committee, that a delegation came over to the bank one day and Brigadier General Raymond Davis, the most highly decorated Marine in the United States, had accepted the job as Executive Director of the Georgia State Chamber of Commerce, and Jasper Dorsey, the President of Southern Bell/BellSouth, now AT&T, was with him. My secretary came in and said, 'Miss Crawford, there's a delegation out here to see you,' and I said, 'A delegation? Who in the world would be coming to see me?'"

"When they came in and got settled, General Davis said, 'Miss Crawford, as you know, the Georgia State Chamber of Commerce has been looking for years for the right woman to become a Director of the Georgia State Chamber of Commerce, who is most representative of all women in Georgia, both business and professional, and you are that lady, and we want you to serve on the Georgia State Chamber of Commerce Board of Directors.' The first and only woman at that time. That was in 1972. So I did, for three years."

"That was also when I became a member of the Georgia Chamber of Commerce, when I went on the Board in about 1972. When I took that job, I was the only woman. At the time, they would meet sometimes at men's hunting clubs in South Carolina, and the wives of the members had never even been permitted to go. I knew that was going to be a problem, and I didn't want it to be, so before we went, I said, 'Don't worry about a place for me to stay in the lodge because my twin and my dog and I will be staying in a motel." I didn't want it to be a problem, and I didn't want the men to get in trouble at home since their wives hadn't been permitted to come. I wasn't one of those pushy women who insisted that I stay in the lodge with all those men. It might have been nice, but I didn't insist on it."

"We were never ones who wanted to invade a man's territory. If they want to have this or that club, that's all right. We weren't not going to be suing them to gain admittance. We never wanted to be anywhere we were not wanted. Just like a few years ago over at the Masters. I think women should be permitted to play, if they can play at that level. I don't think they should be excluded. And I think they should be members of the club, in spite of Mr. Hootie Johnson."[19]

Throughout their lives, the Crawford sisters have been part of church. From their earliest upbringing until the present, missing church on a Sunday was virtually unheard of, no matter where they were. In their home churches—there were two really, Atlanta and Temple—they were as active as any members, and they worked in concert with other churches and denominations on all manner of community service projects. Long before the term "faith-based initiative" became the stuff of political and social debate, Ruth and Ruby Crawford, never ones to proselytize, preferred to allow their lives and their treatment of other people speak their faith for them. They lived what they believed and believed what they lived, all the while working as hard as they could at any task that needed doing.

—

Single girls like to get the church
before the "hymns" give out.

"I guess we've been kind of fixtures at Peachtree Road United Methodist Church," Ruth recalled. "We've been full-time members ever since Mother and Daddy died in 1968. When they were living, we used to go out and spend every weekend with them. Nothing kept us from going to Temple to spend the weekend with our mother and daddy, unless we were off on a trip. If we were going on a trip, we'd go to Temple the night before we left and then we would see them the night we got back, and we'd call them every day. For a long time, after we joined at Peachtree Road, we could go to church here to the early service and still make it out to Temple where we went on the weekends to the family home out there."

"Outreach has always been our favorite," Ruby said, "helping others, the homeless and hungry and all that we do at church. Every March we do a Great Day of Service and primarily my choice has been to have parties for people in nursing homes, the elderly. We have bingo and brunches in which we feed them all and have bingo parties and buy prizes for them and have a pianist playing and we just entertain them while we are there."

"Every year," Ruby announced, "I do about a thousand sandwiches for Must Ministries out in Marietta. I'm the Chairman of that. We don't just do the ham and cheese, we do chicken salad, pimento cheese, and all kinds of sandwiches for the homeless and hungry. I like to make good thick ones. Mine are more the "Dagwood" type. I mean a real sandwich. I've threatened several times to have a course in sandwich making for our members, but I haven't gotten around to doing it, yet."

Each year, WXIA Television Channel 11 in Atlanta recognizes ten people who are contributing significantly to community service, making life better, helping the poor and disadvantaged in any way they can to make the community a better place to live, and who do so without any hope or effort given to being recognized for it. Ruth and Ruby were given that award in 2004.

"We were also inducted into the Atlanta Hospitality Hall of Fame. We were the only women at that time. Our pictures hang prominently in the Georgia World Congress Center. Have you ever seen a picture of that stained glass window down at the Senior Citizens Center on John Wesley Drive? It's all done in red, white, and blue. That's us. We were the first women in the Atlanta Convention and Business Bureau Hospitality Hall of Fame, too."

In October 2008, Ruby was invited by the American Bar Association to become a Fellow of the American Bar Association. "It is just the highest honor. When I read the lovely letter they sent me," Ruby observed laughing, "I thought I must be reading someone else's mail. But it was real, and I am just so honored."

In April 2004, Ruth and Ruby Crawford appeared on the Kennesaw State University program *Meet the President*, hosted by Dr. Betty Siegel, then-president of the University, who introduced Ruth and Ruby by listing their many accomplishments, beginning with their careers as bankers, lawyers, and accountants. Dr. Siegel also pointed out that Ruth and Ruby had been "honored by the Court of the Most Gracious Ladies of Georgia in their meeting in Columbus, Georgia. They were presented with the Deen Day Smith Tribute of Service Award for their contributions to others. They have been in the Atlanta Hospitality Hall of Fame."

On March 24, 2004, Ruth and Ruby Crawford were honored by Kennesaw State University's RTM Institute for Leadership, Ethics & Character at the fourth Annual Phenomenal Women's Conference. The twins from Temple, Georgia each received the Jeanne B. Cook Phenomenal Woman Award.

Reflecting on that award, Ruth recalled, "One of the questions we were asked when we were out at Kennesaw State was if we thought people were different today. I said that I didn't think people were as courteous or as mannerly as they once were. With things like road rage and people not wanting anyone to get ahead of them at a traffic light, they just don't seem to care what anyone thinks. That's a small thing, but it tells a lot. It's such a shame, because life is so much easier, so much better, if you have good attitude, think of others, and keep a smile on your face."

Ruby added, "There is a lack of civility that I think is one of our major problems. People are just not as considerate of one another like they used to be. We find that very disturbing."

"We weren't raised like that, not at all."

Chapter Thirteen

Gracious Ladies

gra·cious ('grā-shəs) *adj.* 1. Characterized by kindness and warm courtesy. 2. Characterized by tact and propriety. 3. Of a merciful or compassionate nature. 4. Courteous; indulgent. 5. Characterized by charm or beauty; graceful. 6. Characterized by elegance and good taste. 7. Archaic. Enjoying favor or grace; acceptable or pleasing. — gra·cious·ly *adv.* — gra·cious·ness *n.*

American Heritage Dictionary
of the English Language, Third Edition

W e were always friends with President Carter, even before the Peanut Brigade, since he was in the legislature here in Georgia. That's when we first met him, and then as Governor. We are good friends of the President and his family. I still am. I went to Crested Butte February first through the fifth [2006] with them. I just got back. Every year for fourteen years they have invited Ruth and me to go on that winter ski family vacation trip where they include other people. Last year Ruth and I said, 'Oh, it's just so expensive.' We didn't ski. We would go for the people we love, the camaraderie, and to see the Peanut Brigaders and old friends, so we said, 'Maybe next year.' So this was the next year, and about two or three weeks before time to go I got to thinking seriously and thought Ruth and I should both be going, but Ruth isn't with me anymore, so since Ruth can't go, I'm going to go myself. And I did."

"We had the best time. We had a chartered Delta jet and a lot of the Delta officials went with us. I'm telling you, the champagne started flowing from the time we left the runway and Jimmy came through the plane shaking hands with everybody. When he got to me, he kissed me twice. I guess one was for Ruth. That was so sweet. I've never seen so much snow in all my life. It was about fifteen inches deep on all the roof tops. The Mayor of Crested Butte took me on a sightseeing trip that I thought was kind of funny, because sightseeing in snow, if you're not used to it, looks the same on this street as on another street. All you could see was snow. On Saturday night we had a big banquet. We took over Club Med out there. There was a big sign up saying 'Closed for a Private

Party February 1–5.' Saturday night all those three hundred people sang Happy Birthday to me, because February 5 was our birthday. They had a big birthday cake. It was a big angel food cake with whipped cream and strawberries. They only put three candles on it, because if they'd put them all, it would have melted all that snow out in Crested Butte. They certainly didn't want to do that. I cut the first piece and gave it to the President and the second for Rosalyn."

"One of the things that I thought was so interesting Saturday night was that they always have a big auction to raise money for the Carter Center. As I said, there were about three hundred people including a Royal Highness from Iran, who I think maybe might have been the son of the late Shah of Iran. There were also many people who contribute to the Carter Center. It was just a wonderful delegation of interesting people from everywhere. The Saturday night auction was full of all of kinds of things that had been donated, along with things from the Carter Library that have been on display for quite some time and were to be replaced, and also gifts that had been given to the Carters. As you know, the President has started painting, in addition to his woodworking and book writing and all the travels that he does observing elections and trying to bring peace and hope and medical attention to all the world, curing diseases–particularly River Blindness, Guinea Worm, and AIDS.

President Carter had painted a scene of the Japanese Garden at the Carter Presidential Center and it was auctioned and sold for $40,000, even though he's an amateur painter. He's just started painting. He also built a cabinet, like a kitchen cabinet. It had three shelves and two doors down underneath and it was highly polished. He made it out of persimmon wood. The persimmon tree had been across a little creek on that property for years, and they got that tree out and had it all done up so that they could use the lumber. They started the bids at $300,000 and John Moore from San Diego, who was seated second from me at our table bid One Million Dollars for that cabinet! They didn't ask for any more bids after that. I don't know how far above a million it might have gone if they hadn't stopped. I was flabbergasted that they raised $1,710,000 for the Carter Center. I later saw the President on television talking about the cabinet, and he said the man who owned the tree made golf clubs and had saved it for that purpose, but then everyone had switched to metal clubs and so persimmon was no longer desirable and he got the tree. We had a great time out there."

—

It's a shame that when you finally get your life together,
you forget where you put it.

Of all the accolades, awards, and attention Ruth and Ruby have so justifiably earned throughout their lives, the most important and most cherished for the Crawford sisters is their induction into an organization known as The Gracious Ladies of Georgia.

—

The reason a woman's mind is cleaner
than a man's is that she changes it more often.

"The Gracious Ladies of Georgia was begun by Roselle Fabiani, a local television personality in Columbus, Georgia. She did the *With Roselle in Columbus* television program every day for years. We went to her—I want to say ten thousandth broadcast in Columbus."

"When she founded The Gracious Ladies of Georgia, Roselle's aim was to recognize women who have contributed so much to helping other women without any expectation of remuneration or recognition for themselves, making life more beautiful for other people. That became the goal for The Gracious Ladies for all the years of its existence. We were so proud to be selected, and we've been members for twenty-nine years."

"We were invited to join in 1977, and we attended every meeting for twenty-eight years. They were the most beautiful affairs that you can ever imagine. There's nothing that we have ever been to in Atlanta, or anywhere else for that matter, that was more beautiful than a meeting of The Gracious Ladies of Georgia."

"Roselle did it, she built The Gracious Ladies. She was the most gracious lady."

"Roselle passed away in March of 2005, and The Gracious Ladies of Georgia have disbanded now. They had the final salute to her and all the Gracious Ladies in September of 2005. They, those who were members, are all Gracious Ladies, but there won't be any additional ones."

"Ruth was in the hospital when the final salute was held and I was hoping—and even thought the doctors were going to let her out—that we were going to go. I even took my party clothes to the hospital, hoping to go, and hoping they were going to let her go, but she wasn't able to. I just wish so much that she could have gone to that with me."

"I would guess Roselle and Ruth are up there in Heaven comparing notes on me now, which might be a little dangerous for me."

Epilogue

The Race

Do you not know that in a race all the runners run, but
only one gets the prize? Run in such a way as to get the
prize. Everyone who competes in the games goes into
strict training. They do it to get a crown that will not
last; but we do it to get a crown that will last forever.

I Corinthians 9:24–25

For nearly every Fourth of July running of the Peachtree Road Race, Ruth
and Ruby Crawford stood in front of The Peachtree Road United Methodist
Church in their patriotic red, white, and blue. On July 4, 2005 they took up
their traditional posts out in front of the Church to encourage and cheer on
the athletes and to greet the sisters' many friends and admirers. The 2005 race
was the last one Ruth and Ruby attended together. But Ruby has continued the
tradition doing double duty for herself and Ruth and carrying on with typical
Crawford grace.

In 2002, Atlanta elected its first woman mayor, Shirley Franklin, whose
promise to clean up the city's government and make it more responsive and
efficient took her into office by a huge margin.

It does not stretch credulity to suggest that the way to the Mayor's Office for
Shirley Franklin was in some small measure excavated and paved by women like
Ruth and Ruby Crawford, who, without movements, rallies, demonstrations,
or strikes, became leaders and inspirations in the community. Neither Ruth
nor Ruby would likely see things quite that way, as theirs has never been the
habit of taking credit or patting their own backs. But in the span of a few
decades the doors to offices, jobs, and other opportunities opened to women,
and it was hard-working women of enterprise and enduring grace embodied
in Ruth and Ruby Crawford who helped to open those doors and led the way
as others walked and still others ran through them.

It is important to note that while Ruth and Ruby were able to recall every
award and honor that came their way, they did so appreciatively, reverently,
and matter-of-factly, remembering them as simply part of their life adventure.
As often as not, if any pride were shown, it was Ruth who would brag on Ruby
and Ruby who would boast about Ruth. They never seemed impressed by their
own specialness, but took it as a by-product of their upbringing, service, and

faith. They may have broken down professional barriers, but more important than that, they are just incredibly nice, generous women with great wit and intelligence, and charm to burn.

Every now and then someone extraordinary comes along and changes the world into a better place than it was when he or she arrived. In Ruth and Ruby Crawford, the world got lucky, twice.

Acknowledgments

Few, if any, writing projects are solo efforts, and this one certainly is not.

Most of all I would like to thank Ruby Crawford, who is no longer with us in what seems a sad and inequitable loss to everyone who knew and loved her. In the summer of 2008 Ruby, even though she was battling increasing health issues and her eyesight was failing, worked tirelessly with me on many hot Atlanta afternoons to discuss and review the manuscript of this book, to identify the hundreds of pictures, and to add anecdotes and stories that richened this account of the lives of the two very energetic, compassionate, and remarkable twin sisters. Ruby herself, in her inimitable style, compiled a handwritten list of some 300 names of friends throughout Atlanta, Georgia, and the country that she (and Ruth) wanted at the celebration launching this book. While Ruby did not live to see the finished book, she did read every major draft, including the final manuscript, and reported that she very much liked what she read.

I want to thank Ruth Crawford and Larry Lowenstein, who also are not with us at the completion of this work but whose contributions were and are invaluable. They are missed by all who knew and loved them. Without their assistance, confidence, and abundant contributions, this book could never have been written. Ruth, then in failing health herself, is especially to be thanked for "digging out" the dozens of photo albums that were all neatly stacked behind the driver's seat in the back of her Chrysler.

Special thanks to Dr. Betty Siegel, Distinguished Chair of the Siegel Institute for Leadership, Ethics and Character and President Emeritus of Kennesaw State University, who conceived this idea and set people and events into motion so this book could be written. Thanks too to Dr. Laura Dabundo and Ellen Taber of Kennesaw State for their suggestions, comments, editing, and encouragement.

I also want to specially thank Holly S. Miller, of the Kennesaw State University Press, publisher of this book, for her industry and artistry in designing this book and her infinite patience in the face of all manner of obstacles and setbacks. Thanks as well to Barbara Calhoun, Dean of Continuing Education at Kennesaw State, and her staff and colleagues, whose hard work and dedication to this book is born solely out of their love for Ruth and Ruby. Barbara particularly deserves special thanks for marshaling resources and people and rallying all concerned in this enterprise.

A special thank you is due to all my writing teachers in the Master of Arts in Professional Writing program at KSU. Drs. Greg Johnson, Don Russ, Rich Welch, and Bill Hill, and most especially Dr. Tony Grooms and Dr. Susan Hunter, each in his or her own unique and effective way taught me that writing, no matter what the subject, is a collaborative effort but is only finally accomplished in solitary confinement.

Thanks too are due to my aunt Mary Cooper, who was kind enough to transcribe hours of recorded conversations. I would also like to thank my test readers, among them my dear friend, Larry McDonald, who waded through the first few very rough drafts; my step-mother Betty Jo Wilkinson, Ph.D., whose expertise and insight were very helpful; and my friends Betsy Bearden and Debra Thomas and again my aunt, Mary Cooper, each of whom donated time reading and appraising passages of this book and doing so without complaint or flinching more than a few times. Thanks also to Bill Volkmer for contributions from his very extensive photographic archive of Atlanta's streetcars and trolleys.

I want to most especially thank my editor, Lindsie Tucker, whose patience, skill, and enthusiasm for this book is as unparalleled as her friendship is treasured. Thank you, Lindsie.

To John Ferrell, Hank Thompson, Jo Carter, Mike Fuhrman, and the rest of the wonderfully friendly and energetic staff at Mary Mac's Tea Room, thank you all very much for your hospitality and for sharing not only your great admiration for and wonderfully funny stories about the Crawford twins, but also for providing photographs of the twins from Mary Mac's walls, some of which appear in this book. Many thanks also to William Johnson, who fed and entertained me during my visits to Mary Mac's and who shared with me his old family recipe for tomato gravy, an especially big hit with my wife Terry and equally delicious on cornbread or white rice. I would also like to thank the folks at The Varsity and the Gordy family for their fine hospitality and to congratulate them on their eighty-second year in business.

And again to Ruth and Ruby Crawford, thank you for generously allowing me into your lives, your family, and your history and for cheerfully sharing with me your experiences, your humor, your faith, your energy, and your heart.

I would be remiss were I not to thank my children, whose encouragement and excitement over this project and their dad always keeps my tanks full. I would also like to thank my son Derek and my daughter-in-law Shay for Sam, who is a whirlwind of smart, funny, and curious, and my daughter Adrianne and my son-in-law Justin for Jake, the original irresistible force and immovable object all rolled into one great kid.

Finally, my warmest thanks are due to my dear and patient wife, Terry, for time and again reading and correcting the tiniest of details in the many drafts of this book and for putting up with my grousing about never getting it right. She has been steadfast throughout this endeavor, just as she has loved and supported me in anything I am doing.

—Neil Wilkinson

Endnotes

1. The capital of and largest city in Georgia, Atlanta is located in the northwest part of the state. When Union General William Tecumseh Sherman began his destructive and fiery march to the sea, to, as he said, "make Georgia howl," the city was burned. Rapidly rebuilt and adopting the Phoenix as its symbol, it became the state capital in 1877, and continues its growth unimpeded.

    Atlanta's first three mayors were elected under the banner of the Rowdy Party, more formally known as the "Free and Rowdy Party." Then in 1850 Jonathan Norcross won the mayoral election as the candidate from the Moral Party. The Atlanta Mayor Norcross served was, like many towns on the more western frontier of America, divided between solid citizens interested in a quiet, law-abiding, prosperous town and those whose name, in this case the "Rowdies," vied for a very different way of life. When Norcross assumed the office of mayor, Atlanta had nearly fifty establishments with pouring licences, that is, they were bars. There was also a very active red light district with perhaps as many as forty establishments. Mayor Norcross, with the zeal that only the son of a preacher can muster, created enough heat and discomfort for the Rowdies that they moved out of Atlanta to a place called Slabtown on the present-day site of Grady Memorial Hospital. The district took its name from the fact that it was constructed from the ground up with slabs of wood from Mayor Norcross's sawmill.

    Before becoming Atlanta, the city was first known as Terminus. That name indicated only a small spot on the map to the east of the Chattahoochee River. In 1836, when the General Assembly voted to build the Western and Atlantic Railroad to join the Georgia Railroad that ran from Augusta and the Macon & Western that linked Macon and Savannah, routes west opened through Terminus. Initially, Terminus was located far north of what is now downtown Atlanta, close to the city center of Norcross. In 1837, after Terminus, in a cost-saving measure, was moved to Montgomery Ferry, later renamed DeFoors Ferry, the General Assembly set the city center, designated by mile marker zero, in an area where the Georgia World Congress Center now stands. The flat terrain there was much more suited to railroad operations than the hillier northern location. Atlanta's first retail establishment, a general store, was opened in the area by a man named John Thrasher and his partner, a gentleman identified only as Mr. Johnson.

    As the railroad was built, Terminus grew to the point that in the five years since the zero mile marker was set the town boasted six buildings and counted thirty residents. Soon a train depot appeared and the town became known as Marthasville, named after the daughter of former Georgia Governor, Representative, and Senator Wilson Lumpkin. The town was officially incorporated on December 23, 1843 and its name changed from Terminus to Marthasville. After a few other names were suggested,

Chief Engineer of the Georgia Railroad, J. Edgar Thomson, proposed that the town be named "Atlantica-Pacifica" in recognition of its railroading roots and continental aspirations. That somewhat cumbersome name was shortened to Atlanta.

By Act 109 of the Georgia General Assembly the political subdivision of Atlanta was established and the town named Marthasville became Atlanta the day after Christmas in 1845.

> An Act [of the General Assembly]
> AN ACT to change the name of Marthasville, in DeKalb county, to that of Atlanta; also, to change the election precinct now held at the house of Charner Humphries, known as the Whitehall precinct, to Atlanta.
> * SECTION 1. Be it enacted by the Senate and House of Representatives of the State of Georgia, in General Assembly met, and it is hereby enacted by the authority of the same, That from and after the passage of this act, the name of Marthasville, in DeKalb county, shall be changed to that of Atlanta.
> * SEC. 2. And be it further enacted by the authority aforesaid, That the election precinct now established by law at the house of Charner Humphries, known as the Whitehall precinct, be and the same is hereby changed to Atlanta.
> * SEC. 3. And be it further enacted by the authority aforesaid, That all laws and parts of laws militating against this act, be and the same are hereby repealed.
> * Approved, December 26th, 1845

Three days later, the Act was law, and Atlanta was officially born. In 1847, Atlanta's city charter was approved, and its first election of city councilmen and a mayor was held, the winners of those elections taking office in January of 1848.

After his term as Atlanta's mayor, Norcross was an instrumental and driving force in expanding the railroad presence in Atlanta that established the city as a transportation center, foreshadowing the city's role when aviation made its debut. By the time of the Civil War, Mayor Norcross occupied the role of citizen emeritus. He was in his mid-50s and not of an age when military service was a logical step. Mayor Norcross was among the citizens who negotiated the surrender of Atlanta to the Union Army that had surrounded the city, having captured Marietta, Roswell, Lawrenceville, Decatur, Morrow, Jonesboro, Douglasville, and others towns that were situated astride the rail lines that fed into Atlanta. The City of Norcross, Georgia, is named in honor of Mayor Jonathan Norcross.

2. According to The Varsity's official history, "The original Varsity was opened in 1928 on a 70' X 120' lot with a white picket fence by a man named Frank Gordy; a man with a $2000 nest egg and 'million dollar taste buds.' Through his dedication to freshness, superior quality, advanced technology, and serving the best food fast, he gained a reputation that is known worldwide. The Varsity has hosted well known people from the entertainment industry, the sports industry, the Governor's mansion, the White House, as well as visitors from all over the globe. Through Frank Gordy's determination, the original Varsity has grown into a two-story 'Lunching Pad' and there are now 6 sister locations. The Varsity has become an Atlanta institution known and loved by all." http://www.thevarsity.com/history.php

3. Loew's Grand Theater was built in 1893 and originally named DeGive's Grand Opera House by its builder Laurent DeGive, a Belgian businessman. The theatre was located on Peachtree Street at the intersection of Peachtree and Pryor. It was famous for its incandescent stage lighting, a novelty in Atlanta at that time. Loew's leased the theater and converted it into a movie house, covering the ornate decorations with drywall. The theatre burned in 1978 and in 1982 the site became the headquarters of Georgia-Pacific.

4. Jacob's Pharmacy was a fixture in Atlanta for many years. Its Jacob's Pharmacydrug No. 1 (there was a chain of 18 stores), at the intersection of Peachtree and Marietta Streets, was a "venerable Five Points institution" since 1897. It is the first place where Coca-Cola was served in Atlanta, and was a favorite of Atlantans and visitors to the city for many years. Store No. 1 continued in operation until its closing June 1, 1963.

5. Mary McKinsey opened Mary Mac's Tea Room in 1945 after realizing she could make money from her fine Southern food. At the time, women didn't run restaurants. Instead they were hostesses of Tea Rooms, a much more genteel past time. Atlanta's streetcars were still running in those days, and the restaurant was strategically located on the Ponce de Leon Avenue line not far from the Crackers baseball home and just down the street from the Fox Theater. So popular were Tea Rooms in Atlanta that at one time there were sixteen in operation. Mary Mac's is now the only one left.

When Margaret Lupo bought Mary Mac's, she expanded the restaurant to its current size. Like Mary McKinsey, Ms. Lupo was a smart, hard-working businessperson with a love for Southern cuisine. Ms. Lupo transformed Mary Mac's from a small Tea Room to one of the most popular restaurants in the South. Throughout the restaurant, the walls are covered with hundreds of pictures of Mary Mac's many friends, including Ruth and Ruby Crawford.

All this was accomplished at a time when there were few women in business and obtaining financing was difficult, if not impossible. Current owner, John Ferrell, Jr., bought the Tea Room in 1994 and continues to run Mary Mac's just as it has been run since the beginning. *Mary Mac's Tea Room* http://www.marymacs.com/History/tabid/53/Default.aspx

6. The Henry Grady Hotel was designed and built in 1924 by Atlanta architect G. Lloyd Preacher (who also designed Atlanta's City Hall, the ill-fated Winecoff Hotel, and the Medical Arts Building at 394 Peachtree Street, NW) at the site of the old Georgia Governor's Mansion at 210 Peachtree Street, NW where it intersects what is now Andrew Young International Boulevard (formerly Cain Street). The hotel had thirteen floors and fifty-five guest rooms, along with the luxurious Paradise Room. The building was eventually taken down in 1972 to make way for the Westin-Peachtree Hotel, the circular shape of which, with its attached glass-enclosed exterior elevator shaft and revolving restaurant on the seventy-third floor, has made it a distinctive mark on the Atlanta skyline ever since.

7. According to the Smyrna, Georgia, Historical and Geneological Society, "In 1941 Isoline Campbell MacKenna converted an existing 1890s-era cabin on her property to a country store to sell preserves and produce grown and produced on her farm. She soon began selling soup and other foods prepared from the recipes of her family's retired cook—Fanny Williams. Demand for the prepared foods grew and in the early 1940s the brick-floored Terrace Room was added and the restaurant, named Aunt Fanny's Cabin, opened. By 1945 the restaurant had established itself as "a place to eat and be seen." The restaurant served authentic Southern-style food, America's oldest recognized cuisine, in a rustic environment …. During its five decades of operation, the restaurant was visited by movie stars, sports figures, politicians, and other notables and celebrities who not only signed the guest book, but left behind many autographed photos that graced the walls. The restaurant … closed [ ] in 1994 … The 1890s cabin and 1940s Terrace Room were moved to the current location in 1998 and refurbished for use as a welcome center … the final owner, donated the historic memorabilia and celebrity photos … to the city of Smyrna" where they are housed in the Smyrna Visitor's Center. Smyrna Historical and Geneological Society http://smyrnahistory.org/welcomecenter.htm

8. Mammy's Shanty was one of Atlanta's finest restaurants in that era. Long since gone, it was located in the area known as Pershing Point where Peachtree Street and West Peachtree Street merge.

9. Rich's policy was to issue a store credit on any returned merchandise, even if the store did not sell it. The belief at Rich's was that people are basically honest and that going the "extra mile" for its patrons would prove beneficial for the company. Not everyone in retailing shared that philosophy, but the growth and popularity of Rich's over the years and the fierce loyalty of its customers were a testament to the effectiveness of Rich's philosophy. To this day it is not at all difficult to find Atlanta

natives or long-time residents who lament or are downright angry at the loss of that revered institution.

10. As a member of the Board of Regents overseeing public higher education in Georgia, Talmadge attempted to have UGA professors, administrators, and members of the Board of Regents fired for harboring what he termed "integrationist" views. The University lost its accreditation for a time and Talmadge lost the then-upcoming race for governor.

11. Roosevelt holds a special place in the hearts of Georgians. The Roosevelt Warm Springs Institute for Rehabilitation was founded in 1927 in Warm Springs, Georgia, by Roosevelt and philanthropist Basil O'Connor to treat people stricken with polio. Roosevelt contracted polio in 1921 and lost use of his legs. The Institute was founded after Roosevelt was told of a boy who regained use of his legs through hydrotherapy. Prior to the war Roosevelt spent quite a lot of time in Warm Springs after discovering that the waters in southern Meriwether County offered relief to his polio-stricken legs. During the war years, Roosevelt was unable to visit the Little White House as often as he would have liked. As the pressures from the war and his failing health took their toll, Roosevelt, in late March of 1945, made his final trip to Warm Springs. On April 12, while preparations were being made for a barbecue and a celebration, Roosevelt died unexpectedly.

12. The term Jim Crow was derived from a character in a song and dance routine that first became popular in 1828 and continued well into the twentieth century in one form or another. The routine titled Jump Jim Crow was first performed in black face by white comedian Thomas Dartmouth (T.D.) "Daddy Jim Crow" Rice. Lyrics were sold to the public by publisher E. Riley beginning in the early 1830s and was purportedly imitative of a song and dance performed by a crippled African in Cincinnati, Ohio, named either Jim Cuff or Jim Crow. It was one of the biggest hits of the 19th century and the images it invoked were perpetuated by Al Jolson, Amos and Andy, and Sherman Helmsley in his little-disguised character George Jefferson. "Jim Crow" in the context used here refers to a series of laws enacted in Southern, border, and other states between 1876 and 1965 that mandated segregation in public facilities under the "separate but equal" doctrine (as set out in Plessey v. Ferguson in 1896) directed at black and other non-white Americans, leading to treatment and accommodations that were inferior to those provided for white Americans in economic, educational, and social matters. The Jim Crow laws segregated public schools, public establishments, public transportation, restrooms, and restaurants. Segregation in public schools was declared unconstitutional by the Supreme Court of the United States in the 1954 case of Brown v. Board of Education. The remaining Jim Crow laws were overridden by the 1964 Civil Rights Act and the 1965 Voting Rights Act.

13. No one really knows where the nickname "Crackers" came from. There is the derogatory term for a poor white Southerner, but there is also the idea that a cracker is someone who gets things done quickly and well. Tim Darnell, in *The Crackers: Early Days of Atlanta Baseball* suggests, "One theory is that the team was named after local farmers who cracked whips over oxen and horses. Another theory is that the name originated from the city's previous team, the Firecrackers." Whatever the origin, the Crackers were the major drawing card, in Atlanta sports. Charles Abner Powell, "[the] colorful and innovative executive" of the team, came up with successful promotional ideas, among them the 'rain check' and 'ladies' day,' that are still observed at ballparks all over the country. From 1901 until 1907, the Crackers played wherever they could find a field around town. Eventually, the team found a home at Ponce de Leon Ballpark, where they stayed until they disbanded. In those days, baseball and baseball parks were segregated. But the Crackers, ever innovative, played three exhibition games against the Brooklyn Dodgers, a team that had made history by putting Jackie Robinson, a black athlete, on its roster. Before a crowd of more than 25,000 on April 10, 1949, the largest ever at Ponce de Leon Park, nearly 14,000 black fans attended. For the first time in Atlanta history black and white athletes took the field in competition with one another in a professional sporting contest. The Crackers dissolved when the Braves came from Milwaukee to Atlanta in 1966.

14. According to the American Bankers Association: "The American Institute of Banking (AIB) is a national organization dedicated to offering professional continuing education and training to bankers ... AIB's national curriculum includes more than 50 programs on a range of banking topics including compliance, corporate banking, management, marketing, sales, and retail banking, plus core courses in accounting, communications, and banking fundamentals ... as building blocks that allow a student to earn AIB diplomas and certificates."

15. The June 1, 1956, Eastern Airlines flight to Montreal, Canada was the first international flight out of Atlanta. In 1957, the first jet flight arrived at Atlanta Municipal, making the short run, as measured by contemporary standards, from Washington, D.C. to Atlanta in under two hours. That same year, construction started on a new terminal designed to handle the crowds of passengers moving into, out of, and through Atlanta. In that era, between noon and 2 p.m. each week day, Atlanta was the busiest airport in the world, a trend that has not abated significantly in more than six decades.

16. The County Unit System in Georgia was used to determine the victor in a primary election. It works a bit like the Electoral College in Presidential Elections. In each county a candidate with the majority vote in that county won the "unit votes, " creating a method of block voting. If no majority emerged, there would be a run-off between the top two candidates, that is, those with the greatest numbers of

votes would compete in a second primary. The system was constructed around the populations of the counties in the State. Of the four hundred and ten votes in 1962, when the method was struck down by the U.S. Supreme Court in *Sanders v. Gray*, the eight counties with the highest populations were allowed six votes apiece, totaling forty-eight votes. The thirty most populous counties after that were in control of four votes each, aggregating to one hundred and twenty votes, and the balance, one hundred and twenty counties had two votes each, for a total of two hundred and forty-two votes. Counties with two votes would have a majority even though they represented only a third of the State's population, violating the Supreme Court found, the "one man, one vote" rule. Eugene Talmadge was a beneficiary of the system when he won the 1946 governor's race, even though he lost by 16,000 popular votes to James Carmichael.

17. Ruth and Ruby appeared in Episode 229 that aired on October 17, 1954. They were in New York at a convention of CPAs and were asked to come on the show.

18. Northside Realty was an Atlanta mainstay and icon in the real estate business from its founding until it merged with Coldwell-Banker Buckhead Brokers in 2002. Howard Chatham founded the company and owned it until 1991. U. S. Senator Johnny Isakson is a former president of Northside Realty. He and his father, Ed, helped grow the company from 1958 forward. Ed Isakson became Northside's chairman and Johnny Isakson became its president 1977.

19. William "Hootie" Johnson is the "Chairman Emeritus" of Augusta National Golf Club. Begun in 1933 by Atlanta golf legend Bobby Jones, Augusta National hosts the Masters. Johnson's most controversial moment as Chairman began in 2002 and continued through the Masters the following April. The controversy began when Johnson received a letter from feminist political activist Martha Burk, Chair of the National Council of Women's Organizations, that stated in part, "We know that Augusta National and the sponsors of the Masters do not want to be viewed as entities that tolerate discrimination against any group, including women."

Mr. Johnson's incendiary reply came in a statement released to the press that "the message delivered [by Martha Burk] to us was clearly coercive. We will not be bullied, threatened, or intimidated. We do not intend to become a trophy in their display case," and that, "there may well come a day when women will be invited to join our membership, but that timetable will be ours, and not at the point of a bayonet."

The ensuing public protest was very small, due to the venue itself and the fact that Washington Road in Augusta that fronts the Club is a main thoroughfare and heavily traveled on a daily basis, especially during Masters week. The Sheriff cited his constitutionally-granted authority to regulate the "time, place, and manner" of any peaceable assembly and issued permits for 120 people, mandating that the site for the protest be in a vacant lot a half-mile from the entrance to Augusta National. That regulatory effort was challenged in court but upheld and the protesters were obliged to follow the Sheriff's directives. Augusta National, while it has allowed women to play the golf course, has not to date admitted any women members, nor have any women been invited to play in the Masters Tournament.

The final chapter was that Augusta National, not wanting any of its traditional sponsors to feel any repercussions from its policy or from the adverse publicity generated by Martha Burk, arranged with CBS Sports to broadcast the Masters "free from commercial interruption." The Club's position was that it could afford to do so, financially and otherwise, and it did.

Bibliography

Census Factfinder [online]. (2008). Retrieved January 24, 2005, from US Census Bureau Web site: http://factfinder.census.gov/home/saff/main.html?_lang=en

Steve Storey. *Georgia Pacific Railway, Railroad History*. Retrieved September 26, 2006, from Georgia's Railroad History & Heritage Web site: www.railga.com/gpacific.html

Welcome to Temple Georgia: About Temple. (2005). Retrieved January 24, 2005, from Temple, GA Web site: http://temple.ofgeorgia.com/local/cityinfo.html

Georgia Humanities Council and the Office of the Govenor. Cities & Counties. (2008). Retrieved January 24, 2005, from the New Georgia Enclyclopedia Web site: http://www.georgiaencyclopedia.org/nge/Categories.jsp?path=CitiesCounties

Testimony Taken by the Joint Select Committee to Inquire Into the Condition of Affairs in the Late Insurrectionary States. Georgia, vol. I. Washington, D.C.: Government Printing Office, 1872. 411–412. Retrieved July 2, 2007, from History Matters Web site: http://historymatters.gmu.edu/d/6225/

Post, E. (1922). *Etiquette in Society, in Business, in Politics and at Home.* New York and London: Funk & Wagnalls 1922 and Bartleby.com 1999 online edition.

Georgia Public Television (Producer), & Kennedy D. (Host). Aired 1999, and 2001. *Lost Atlanta: The Way We Were* ©1994: United States: Georgia Public Broadcasting. (Graciously made available on DVD by Georgia Public Television, 2007.)

History of WSB Radio. (2003) Originally retrieved February 12, 2008 from WSB History Site created and maintained by Mike Cavanaugh until his death December 6, 2008. http://wsbhistory.com Site donated to the Georgia Radio Hall of Fame. *The Georgia Radio Hall of Fame*: http://www.grhof.com A 501(c)(3) Non Profit Organization (Sites not affiliated with Cox Radio, Inc.) *See also: The History of WSB-TV/Channel 2:* http://www.wsbtv.com/station/4043241/detail.html (2009) Retrieved June 7, 2009

Gone With the Wind (1939). Retrieved June 23, 2006, from Filmsite Web Site: http://www.filmsite.org/gone.html

The Official Academy Awards Database. (2009). Retrieved April 30, 2008, from Academy of Motion Pictures Arts and Sciences Web site: http://http://awardsdatabase.oscars.org/ampas_awards/BasicSearchInput.jsp

The Margaret Mitchell House: Its Historical Significance. (2008). Retrieved April 30, 2008, from Margaret Mitchell House, Atlanta History Center Web site: http://www.gwtw.org/mitchellhouse.html

Worthy, L., *Atlanta Premiere of Gone With The Wind.* (1994-2009). Retrieved April 20, 2008, from About North Georgia Web site: http://ngeorgia.com/ang/Atlanta_Premiere_of_Gone_With_The_Wind

Martin, H. H., & Garrett, F. M. (1987). *Atlanta and Environs: A Chronicle of Its People and Events: Years of Change and Challenge 1940–1976, Volume III.* Athens: University of Georgia Press. Knight, L.L.. (2007). *A Standard History of Georgia and Georgians: Volume I.* Athens: Digital Library of Georgia; Document ID: gb01715a. Retrieved June 11, 2007, from Digital Library of Georgia Web site: dlg.galileo.usg.edu/meta/html/dlg/zlgb/meta_dlg_zlgb_gb0175a.html

Hills, T.D. (2006). First National Bank of Atlanta/Wachovia Bank, N.A.. *Business and Industry.* Retrieved March 30, 2008, from The New Georgia Enclylopedia Web site: http://www. georgiaencyclopedia.org/nge/Article.jsp?id=h-1015

Volkmer, Bill. (Copyright holder). (1999). Atlanta Trolley and Streetcar Photos, [Online Image]. Retrieved October 15, 2006, from Bill Volkmer Collection Web Site: http://www.davesrailpix. com/index.html

Lanning-Minchew, K. (2003). Warm Springs. *Cities and Counties.* Retrieved May 11, 2008, from The New Georgia Enclylopedia Web site: http://www.georgiaencyclopedia.org/nge/Article. jsp?id=h-767

Emporis.com: Atlanta, Tall Buildings. (2009). *Henry Grady Hotel.* Retrieved March 22, 2007, from the Emporis Website: http://www.emporis.com/en/wm/bu/?id=henrygradyhotel-atlanta-ga-usa

Downtown, The Henry Grady Hotel. (2009). Retrieved March 22, 2007, from Atlanta Time Machine Web site: http://www.atlantatimemachine.com/downtown/pch210grady.htm

Farrington, S. *Remembering Atlanta in the 60's and 70's: Mammy's Shanty Restaurant.* (2002). Retrieved May 25, 2008, from Wake Atlanta Web site: http://www.wakeatlanta.com/ atlantasidetripsnumber1_0.html

Smyrna Historical and Genealogical Society: *History of Aunt Fanny's Cabin* (2006). Retrieved May 25, 2008, from Smyrna History Org. Web site http://smyrnahistory.org/_welcomecenter.htm

Mary Mac's Tea Room: Atlanta's Dining Room, History. Retrieved May 25, 2008, from Mary Mac's Tea Room Website http://www.marymacs.com/History/tabid/53/Default.aspx

Bailey, M. (2005). Rich's Department Store. *Business and Industry.* Retrieved May 25, 2008, from The New Georgia Enclylopedia Web site: http://www.georgiaencyclopedia.org/nge/Article. jsp?id=h-1888

Sullivan, P. *Civil Rights Movement. Africana: The Encyclopedia of the African and African American Experience*, 2nd Edition. Ed. Kwame Anthony Appiah. Ed. Henry Louis Gates Jr. Retrieved December 20, 2007, from the Oxford African American Studies Center. Sun Oct 07 14:14:48 EDT 2007. http://www.oxfordaasc.com/article/opr/t0002/e0944.

Myrick-Harris, C., Harris, N., *Atlanta in the Civil Rights Movement: Gradualism and Negotiation (1940–1970), Retrenchment & Redirection (1950–1959), Direct Action and Desegregation (1960–1965), the Quest for Black Power (1966–1970).* Retrieved Feb 12, 2008, from Atlanta Regional Council for Higher Education Web site: http://www.atlantahighered.org/civilrights/essay_detail. asp?phase=1

Digital Library of Georgia: Georgia Govenors. (2009). Retrieved March 8, 2008, from GeorgiaInfo Web site: http://www.cviog.uga.edu/Projects/gainfo/gagovs.htm

Henderson, H. P. (Editor), & Roberts, L. R. (Editor). (1988). *Georgia Governors in an Age of Change: From Ellis Arnall to George Busbee.* Athens: University of Georgia Press.

Darnell, T. (2004). *The Crackers: Early Days of Atlanta Baseball.* Athens: Hill Street Press.

Georgia Public Television (Producer), & Kennedy D. (Host). Aired 1999, and 2001. *Lost Atlanta: The Way We Were* ©1994: United States: Georgia Public Broadcasting. (Graciously made available on DVD by Georgia Public Television, 2007.)

aba.com: Professional Development (2009). Retrieved May 25, 2008, from American Bankers Association Web site: http://www.aba.com/Training/default.htm

Cook, J. F. (2005). *The Governors of Georgia, 1754-2004, 3d ed.* Macon: Mercer University Press.

Henderson, Harold Paulk, *M. E. Thompson and the Politics of Succession*, in Georgia Governors in an Age of Change: From Ellis Arnall to George Busbee, ed. Harold P. Henderson and Gary L. Roberts (Athens: University of Georgia Press, 1988).

Rice, B.R., *Government and Politics, Ivan Allen Sr.* (1876–1968). (2004). Retrieved December 20, 2007, from The New Georgia Encyclopedia Web site: www.georgiaencyclopedia.org/nge/Article.jsp?id=h-2785

Legacy of Ivan Allen, Jr., Ivan Allen Jr. Timeline. (2009). Retrieved December 20, 2007, from Georgia Tech Ivan Allen Collee of Liberal Arts Web site: http://www.iac.gatech.edu/about-us/legacy-of-iv

Coar, S., *40th Anniversary of the Desegregation of the University of Georgia, January 9, 2001* (2001). Retrieved December 2, 2007, from University of Georgia Web site: www.uga.edu/news/desegregation/history/index_firsts.html

John Wesley Dobbs (2005). Retrieved December 2, 2007, from the New Georgia Encyclopedia Web site: http://www.georgiaencyclopedia.org/nge/ArticlePrintable.jsp? id=h-103

Galloway, T.H., *Ivan Allen Jr. (1911–2003).* (2004). Retrieved December 20, 2007, from The New Georgia Encyclopedia Web site: http://www.georgiaencyclopedia.org/nge/ArticlePrintable.jsp?id=h-1382

BBC Home, On this Day 3 June, 1962: *130 die in Paris air crash, Atlanta Arts group killed.* (1962). Retrieved December 20, 2007, from BBC News Online: http://news.bbc.co.uk/onthisday/hi/dates/stories/june/3/newsid_3007000/3007265.stm

The Phoenix Society of Atlanta, *History of the Phoenix Society.* (2008). Retrieved December 20, 2007, from Pheonix Atlanta.Org: http://www.phoenixatlanta.org/history.html
Abrams, A. U. (2002) *Explosion at Orly: The Disaster That Transformed Atlanta.* Atlanta: Avion Press.

Moser, C. (Writer/Director) *The Day Atlanta Stood Still,* (Atlanta: Georgia Public Television, 2001), video.

Rooney, D.R., History and Archaeology, *Orly Air Crash of 1962*. (2003). Retrieved December 20, 2007, from New Georgia Encyclopedia Web site: http://www.georgiaencyclopedia.org/nge/Article.jsp?id=h-1103

The Varsity, Our History. (2007). Retrieved March 11, 2007, from The Varsity Web site: http://www.thevarsity.com/history.php

Schwartz, Maryln, *A Southern Belle Primer or Why Princess Margaret Will Never Be A Kappa Kappa Gamma*. (1991 Broadway Books, New York.)

Galloway, Tammy Harden, "The Three Dollar Tag" 1995. "Tribute of The Masses And A Champion of The People: Eugene Talmadge And The Three Dollar Tag." The Georgia Historical Quarterly 79, no. 3 (Fall), 673-684.

Digital Library of Georgia, Historical Information about Georgia Governors, Historical Roster of the Governors of Georgia (Secretary of State); Term of office for Georgia governors, 1777-present (chart). (2009). Retrieved December 2, 2007, from GeorgiaInfo Web site: http://www.cviog.uga.edu/Projects/gainfo/govhist.htm

Coldwell Banker Buckhead Brokers Northside Realty to merge, Atlanta Business Chronicle: Tuesday, January 29, 2002.

Georgia Chambers of Commerce Directory. (2007). Retrieved December 11, 2007, from West Georgia University Web site: http://www.westga.edu/~mktreal/chamber

Stevens, A. & Fecht, J., *US Mayors, Shirley Franklin Mayor of Atlanta*. (2008). Retrieved November 10, 2007, from City Mayors Web site: http://www.citymayors.com/usa/atlanta.html

Page Student Teacher Achievement Recognition, Selection of State PAGE STAR Winners. (2008). Retrieved December 20, 2007, from PAGE Foundation Web site: http://www.ciclt.net/pagefoundation/star/selection.html

U. S. Chamber of Commerce: http://www.uswcc.org/

Augusta Defends Male Only Members Policy (2007): *Controversy at Augusta National*. Retrieved March 9, 2007, from Golf Today, This Year's News Stories. (1999-2009)) http://www.golftoday.co.uk/news/yeartodate/news02/augusta5.html

Peachtree Road United Methodist Church, Our Story. (2008): Retrieved May 22, 2008, from Peachtree Road United Methodist Church: http://www.prumc.org/index.php?option=com_content&view=article&id=38&Itemid=92

Lowenstein, L. (Creator/Producer) & Siegel. B.L. (Host), (2004). *Meet the President* [Television Broadcast]. United States: Kennesaw State University

About the Author

Neil Wilkinson, a practicing attorney for over seventeen years holds, in addition to degrees in business and law, a Master's Degree in Professional Writing from Kennesaw State University (KSU). He is also an Adjunct Professor of Business Law at the Kennesaw State's Michael J. Coles College of Business.

Wilkinson has published articles in legal and general interest periodicals, as well as poetry and short fiction in regional publications. Wilkinson has completed two novels, *A Day in the Life of A Reasonable Man*, a picaresque farce involving a fussy, overly-grammatical everyman who dislikes being interrupted, who finds himself the plaintiff in a lawsuit against the most powerful televangelist in America, and *Laughing Academy*, a psychological/legal suspense novel, he has other novels in various states of construction. Currently occupying his time are *Pinball in the House of the Lord*, a tapestry of the modern tendency to blur the distinctions between spiritual searching and economic well-being, and *Friday Nights in the American Fall*, a deeply drawn sketch of the privileges of golden-boy athletes.

Running on Full: The Story of Ruth and Ruby Crawford is the biography of Ruth and Ruby Crawford, two remarkable Georgia twin sisters who were instrumental in breaking through many of the glass ceilings encountered by women in mid-twentieth-century America, in such diverse fields as law, accounting, politics, and real estate. Published by the Kennesaw State University Press in the Spring of 2010.

LaVergne, TN USA
10 October 2010

200223LV00004B/3/P